Maximising Tutor Time

Tutor time is something that all students have, but how effectively is this time being utilised? This crucial book is a one-stop-shop in effective tutor time practices to lift student attainment, improve behaviour, boost attendance and so much more.

Written by Nathan Burns, a previous pastoral lead and now educational researcher and teacher trainer, this book will guide you through eight different areas, ranging from messaging to wellbeing, providing high-quality strategies that can be easily incorporated into a tutor programme to support the academic and personal growth of students. Chapters cover:

- Messaging including assemblies and workshops
- Key events and how to build these into the school year
- Creativity
- The brain and learning
- Enrichment activities
- Interventions
- Current affairs
- Wellbeing and health

Packed with strategies that will support your routines, curriculum and pedagogies, this is essential reading for busy classroom teachers, Heads of Year and Senior Leaders.

Nathan Burns is a highly respected teacher educator, supporting schools across the UK in developing their teachers and outcomes for students. He is an expert in the area of metacognition, having written two books on the theory, but also on developing effective pastoral systems and MAT provision.

Maximising Tutor Time

Lift Attainment, Improve Behaviour, Boost Attendance

Nathan Burns

Routledge
Taylor & Francis Group

LONDON AND NEW YORK

Cover image: © Getty Images. Cover design: Jo Steer.

First published 2025
by Routledge
4 Park Square, Milton Park, Abingdon, Oxon OX14 4RN

and by Routledge
605 Third Avenue, New York, NY 10158

Routledge is an imprint of the Taylor & Francis Group, an informa business

British Library Cataloguing-in-Publication Data
A catalogue record for this book is available from the British Library

Library of Congress Cataloging-in-Publication Data
Names: Burns, Nathan, author.
Title: Maximising tutor time: lift attainment, improve behaviour, boost attendance / Nathan Burns.
Description: Abingdon, Oxon; New York, NY: Routledge, 2025. | Includes index.
Identifiers: LCCN 2024057578 (print) | LCCN 2024057579 (ebook) |
ISBN 9781032997612 (hardback) | ISBN 9781032997605 (paperback) |
ISBN 9781003605881 (ebook)
Subjects: LCSH: Tutors and tutoring. | Curriculum planning.
Classification: LCC LC41 .B87 2025 (print) | LCC LC41 (ebook) |
DDC 371.39/4—dc23/eng/20250213
LC record available at https://lccn.loc.gov/2024057578
LC ebook record available at https://lccn.loc.gov/2024057579

ISBN: 978-1-032-99761-2 (hbk)
ISBN: 978-1-032-99760-5 (pbk)
ISBN: 978-1-003-60588-1 (ebk)

DOI: 10.4324/9781003605881

Typeset in Optima
by codeMantra

Contents

Introduction   1

1   Messaging   6

2   Events of the Year   28

3   Creativity Section   44

4   The Brain and Learning   57

5   Interventions   73

6   Enrichment   92

7   Current Affairs   101

8   Wellbeing   113

    Conclusion   124

    Index   *125*

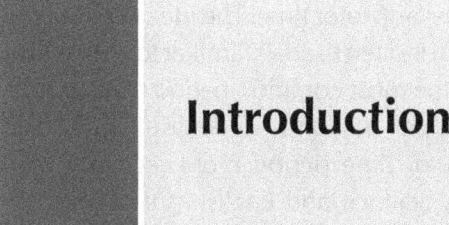

Introduction

In the world of education, we are constantly looking for improvement, whether that be with attainment, attendance, behaviour or something else. Schools continue to improve, building upon the very latest research that we have available to us. Improved knowledge of cognitive load, the importance of retrieval and what effective revision actually looks like are just some of the significant pieces of research to have helped to accelerate the performance of schools and the students who we serve. In many ways, we have run out of 'major' gains that we can make, and instead look towards marginal gains. What are the small tweaks we can make, things we can implement, or even the things that we can remove, which will help to accelerate progress yet further?

However, I believe that there are still major areas left for us to focus on and improve, with one of those being tutor time. Sitting outside of the demands of the National Curriculum, tutor time is used in various different ways across schools. It often provides a 'catch-all' option for the delivery of PSHE, provides a chance for students to receive tutoring, or even to organise parental meetings. Though in these circumstances tutor time becomes helpful, in so much as it provides time to get other things done, it doesn't itself retain a significant value, much beyond a register being taken and a selection of ad hoc activities, such as those outlined above, being completed.

DOI: 10.4324/9781003605881-1

Maximising Tutor Time

Contexts and timetables of schools, both within, and outside of the UK vary, but with one major constant: tutor time. The idea of tutor time (or registration, a synonym which is often used) is familiar to all teachers and students. In fact, it is often the most common period that students have, appearing typically once per day on a student's timetable. In fact, students are often in a tutor time period more regularly than core subjects including Maths, Science and English. Of course, the time allocated to tutor time is not as lengthy as the time allocated to these, or other subjects, but across the course of the week, the cumulative time spent in tutor time is surprisingly large. Twenty minutes per day constitutes almost 2 hours per week, which in many cases is not far off 10% of the time that students spend in school.

We therefore have a subject area – that being 'tutor time' – that constitutes a large part of a student's week. Critically, this means that we have the potential for major improvement. If tutor time is currently an area that is poorly planned, becomes a 'dumping place' for other activities, or is an incoherent group of activities, then this time is not being effectively used to support students as well as it otherwise could be. This is where this book comes in!

The aim of this book is to provide you with a range of activities, which can be utilised to support improvements in a number of areas across school, including behaviour, attendance and overall academic attainment. These high-quality strategies are grouped into eight different areas, which are:

1. Messaging
   A chapter exploring how whole-school expectations around behaviour and attendance, amongst other factors, can be supported and developed through certain activities during tutor time.
2. Events of the Year
   This chapter explore a number of local, national and international events, all of which carry great weight, that you may wish to build in to your tutor programme.

3. Creativity

    These strategies explore ways in which we can foster creativity in our students, providing them with opportunities to learn and develop without academic or exam constraint.

4. The Brain and Learning

    Following a more academic focus, this chapter explores a range of different activities which can be run during tutor time in order to improve the effective study skills of students, and to help develop independent learners.

5. Interventions

    Continuing with the academic theme, this chapter will explore a number of strategies which can allow for interventions to run during tutor time, without them being ad hoc or disruptive.

6. Enrichment

    Tutor time offers an invaluable opportunity to provide students with enriching opportunities. This chapter will explore strategies to support the development of these opportunities.

7. Current Affairs

    To develop a more all rounded student and young individual, it's imperative that we provide our young people with an opportunity to learn about the world around them. This chapter will explore a variety of strategies which do just that.

8. Wellbeing

    This final chapter explores a number of ways in which we can support and safeguard the wellbeing of our young people, so crucial in the education system and world that we live in today.

The aim of these strategies is not to provide a one-size-fits-all solution. It would be impossible to put in place all of these strategies in one go, either! Rather, the range of strategies provided ensures that there will be options for all schools, regardless of their contexts. Equally, each school has its own aims, and its own areas for improvement. For some it may be wellbeing, for other attendance, and so forth. Therefore, which of the eight areas that you place emphasis on is very likely to correspond to the problems that you face and whole-school priorities which you hold.

One recommendation that this book will provide though, is to choose strategies carefully. There are so many high-quality and impactful strategies in this book, but choosing strategies which complement each other, forming a coherent tutor programme, is crucial. At the very start of this introduction, it was noted how tutor time often becomes a dumping group for different activities. This needs to be avoided with the strategies that you choose from this book. Choosing a range of high-quality strategies will not have the desired impact if there is little coherency between them, an underlying aim to them all, or if they are not cemented within a wider curriculum for tutor time. Done correctly, a set of strategies can catapult tutor time from being a dumping ground of necessary activities to an opportunity to drive forward the academic and personal development of the young people in our care.

It should also be noted that this book focuses on a range of quality activities that can be used to form an impactful tutor time curriculum, rather than consider the structure that your tutor programme is in. The length and structure of your tutor time programme are likely pre-determined factors and a key foundation to the school day or structure of the timetable. Rather, the focus here is on making the best decisions for your school, within the constructs that you are within. There will be some strategies within this book that do not suit the context or constraints that you find yourself in. Yet, there will also be many dozens of strategies that do fit the context and constraints in which you find yourselves in, that are contextually sensitive, and can provide a partial, or full solution, to the challenges in which we face in our schools.

With regard to the strategies, the template is simple. Each strategy is provided with a clear heading, followed by a clear explanation of what the strategy is, and what it 'looks like' in person, to support effective implementation. The format is consistent throughout, ensuring easy comparability between strategies, as well as providing you with an easy to 'dip in and out of' blueprint for the perfect tutor time curriculum.

Overall, you will be provided with a clear collection of high-quality strategies, which can be implemented into your tutor time curriculum that combined coherently, and, if implemented effectively, can lead to improved student attainment, improved behaviour and uplifted attendance.

Enjoy!!

Messaging

A key area of importance in schools is to ensure both a consistency of message, as well as opportunities to hold conversations with students around routines, behaviours and attendance. Where consistency is lacking, confusion can reign. What are the updates to the behaviour policy? Where are detentions being held? What are the expectations during a fire drill? All of these messages require consistency, so that expectations can consistently be expected and enforced.

Additionally, tutors need the opportunity to follow up on these areas, too. Should a student consistently be failing to meet these clearly messaged expectations, then conversations need to be held. But when? And how?

This chapter will explore a number of areas where a consistency of message is required, as well as the opportunities that we have to embed messages, practice routines, and hold conversations with students around the expectations that we hold for them.

Overall, then, this chapter looks to provide strategies, which is successfully implemented, can support with an improvement in behaviour by students across school, in contact and non-contact times, as well as during any non-standard events, such as fire drills.

 DOI: 10.4324/9781003605881-2

School Assemblies

School assemblies seem to have been around since the dawn of time. We all had a school assembly when we were at school; all of our students have a school assembly now, too. Too often though, you can walk out of an assembly and wonder what the point is – what couldn't have just been covered if you had stayed in your tutor room with your tutees and passed a few messages on?

However, an assembly is an incredible opportunity to bring together one, or many year groups. First, it ensures a consistency of messaging across all students, as tutors are no longer responsible for passing on messages in their own ways to their tutees. It also ensures that messages do get passed on in the first instance, as we are all too aware that, for many reasons, they can become forgotten in a busy tutor routine.

An assembly also offers the opportunity to practise routines, such as bringing students down to the hall in silence, getting students to line up in alphabetical order and then sit quietly and respectfully as they listen. These opportunities are normally forgotten, but taken seriously, can have massively positive impacts on reinforcing other whole school expectations, especially if you do have policies such as silent corridors or lining up at the end of a break or lunch time.

An assembly also offers the opportunity to deliver core messages to students, especially around culture and expectations. For example, an assembly covering behaviour and the behaviour system ensures that all students have had the same, clear message delivered to them. Equally, and more positively, an assembly could be used to highlight achievements of members of that year group, perhaps in music or sporting fixtures.

Assembly time also offers an opportunity for different members of staff to lead. This means that specialisms, and passions, can shine through. If you have decided on a set of 40 assembly topics that you want delivered over the course of the year (something which I would very much recommend that you do), who, for example, is best to lead the 'Introduction to Politics' assembly, or the one on 'Green Spaces and Recycling'? A member of staff with passion and expertise delivering one of these assemblies is going to be far more intriguing to listen to than a member of SLT 'ticking a box'.

Additionally, an assembly could be hosted by a student, or group of students, such as a student council or tutor group. Once again, these individuals or groups are likely to have areas of interest and expertise that they are wanting to share with others. Planning and then delivering an assembly provides a wonderful opportunity not just to do this, but also to develop a range of soft skills, not least public speaking.

If you are unsure as to the topics that you may wish to cover in your assemblies, then why not begin with your school foci for a year, such as homework or behaviour, as well as any year group foci, such as choosing options or revision. If you are still struggling for ideas, then take a look at the other tutor time ideas in this book, as many of them can be adapted to provide you with a wonderful assembly topic to speak on.

Workshops

Schools are expected to do so much these days. Long gone is the objective of a school just to teach high-quality lessons. Now we have to cover all sorts of pastoral issues, including mental health and PSHE, deal with attendance, cost-of-living consequences, as well as a huge range of other issues.

One way in which schools have tried to deal with this is through the introduction of workshops, either scattered across the school year, on individual weeks or individual days. Workshops can be of high quality, too. Very often, local organisations and charities will send experts into schools, who are well versed in delivering both high-quality and equally intriguing and thought-provoking workshops. All of this is often done for limited cost (e.g. paying for fuel) or no cost at all.

One of the difficulties of this though, is time (when is it not?!). Having these sessions is great, and really helps to support tackling some of these big issues, but losing curriculum time – when there is already so much to do – is far from ideal. And this is where tutor time comes in.

Why not have one tutor time per half-term where students get to go to one of these workshops? They don't need to be long (so don't worry if your tutor time is short), but having them during a tutor time ensures that students can still get access to these high-quality workshops without missing crucial curriculum time. Having these workshops timetabled in every half-term also ensures that they do not get lost amongst a range of other tutor time activities. So, get them booked in, and early at that!

Now that you have seen the benefits of having workshops in your schools, and you have timetabled them in, what are you going to cover in them? Much of this will depend on your school context and community, as the issues you need to cover are typically school centric. Perhaps it is knife crime? Or the dangers of open water? Perhaps racism, drinking, teenage pregnancy or extremism are all issues in your areas? Sit down with your team(s) and find out what the issues are. Speak to your students, and find out what the issues are in *their* community. Then, get in those experts to deliver high-quality, hard-hitting sessions that will support your students no end.

Practising Routines

There really is no better time than a tutor period to practise some crucial routines – especially as so many of these routines often involve just students in a tutor group – for example, lining up after a fire alarm.

Maximising Tutor Time

So often, routines are practised at the beginning of the year, typically on the first day back when there is an 'extended tutor time' on the first morning. Routines also seem to be practised after there have been issues, for example with behaviour on corridors when students are moving around school. However, this is reactive, whereas routine practice can become a proactive move to stop issues from arising in the first instance.

Let's consider some of the routines that can be practised during tutor time (though again, these will vary depending upon the routines that you have in your schools, and how rigid the expectations are. If expectations are tight, then more practice may be needed to get things right!).

First is the fire drill. Why not take some time to practise lining up alphabetically during a tutor time (which can also double up as a good team building exercise, especially where students cannot remember who they follow on the register)? Students can also be made to walk silently down to the area where they would line up and practise a silent line up and register being taken.

Lining up before a lesson can also be practised. Though in some schools students need to line up outside a classroom before entering, including in tutor time, in many schools students 'trickle in' in the mornings, so never have the chance to practise their line up outside a classroom. Again, take some time to practise this routine with students.

Many schools, especially post-COVID, have moved to silent corridors. For highly effective silent corridors, they need to be practised over and over again, so students understand exactly what silence means! Though this will need to be practised at a whole school level, and continually reinforced when it is introduced into a school, there is nothing stopping a tutor group, or tutor groups from a particular year, in doing some extra practice to make sure that they get it right.

Practising routines may seem obvious. However, without taking this time to *teach* students how to meet the expectations of the routine, we are just setting them up to fail. Students ought to have the time to practise, in an environment where they can make mistakes without those behaviours instantly leading to consequences, so that when those behaviours matter, and need to be embedded (e.g. lining up silently before a lesson), they are exceptional clear on what they ought to be doing.

Uniform Checks

Uniform is a perennial issue. As soon as one issue seems to be sorted, there seems to be another one on the horizon. Challenging uniform whilst you're teaching is difficult. You want students to learn, you don't want to have a negative conversation with a student if it can be avoided, and at the end of the day, the priority in a lesson is the content teaching rather than anything else.

Following up on uniform whilst walking a corridor, or doing a duty, is also not easy. As you spend time sorting out that issue, signing diaries or making notes of consequences that you need to add on later, goodness knows how many other incidents are happening as you are distracted.

This is what makes tutor time such an effective time to check in on uniform. Though it does add some workload to a tutor, if uniform issues can be solved at the start of the day, then it will save colleagues a huge amount of work, and potentially 'agro' from students later on (we've all challenged a kid for uniform issues later on in the day who then claims that 'Miss X' or 'Mr Y' didn't have an issue with it so why do you?). Additionally, a tutor is in the best position to monitor recurring issues over uniform that a general teacher, who sees a student a couple of times a week, just wouldn't be in the situation to follow up. This also means that a tutor can spot an issue on, say, a Monday, give the student until Wednesday to rectify it (e.g. sorting out black shoes), and be in a position then on the Wednesday to follow this up again, and take any further actions required, such as issuing consequences or contacting home.

Additionally, and strangely, this can also improve a tutor-tutee relationship. Uniform stems from the idea of consistently high expectations. By ensuring that you, as a tutor, are upholding these very high expectations, and challenging and following up on issues where ever required, you are actually upholding your tutees to the highest standards. Though they may not initially thank you for this, all students are eventually grateful for the high standards and expectations that we give them.

Additionally, with regard to uniform, a tutor, especially one with a positive relationship with their tutees, may be in the best position to glean any required information about home life. For example, if students are constantly in small shoes, or trainers because their shoes haven't been replaced, or trousers that are dirty, a tutor is most likely to be trusted by a tutee to share the reasons for these issues arising. This in turn will allow for a tutor to pass on key information to the safeguarding and pastoral teams, as required and relevant.

Equipment Checks

We've all had a lesson (or every lesson!) where a student asks for a piece of equipment. Whether it be a pen, pencil, ruler, calculator or something else, it doesn't half interrupt a lesson. Not only do you have to stop your teaching, which is a major interruption to your flow, but you then need to track down a spare piece of equipment for the student, or students in question. Moreover, you then need to consider taking collateral (do you need the student to trade their phone for the calculator, just to ensure that you get it back at the end of the lesson?), or some other sort of way to remember who has what piece of equipment. In addition to this is whether you actually have spare equipment in the first place. With budgets tight, equipment low, and its propensity to grow legs and walk away (in student's pockets?) very often you're asking neighbouring students to help out the (equipment) damsel in distress.

Done effectively, tutor time checks on equipment can ensure that this doesn't happen, or at least is greatly reduced. One effective way to do this is with students getting out all required equipment at the door, to show you as they enter, or placing it out on the desk in front of them when they sit down. You can quickly check to see who has what equipment. When you have identified what students are missing, these can be loaned to students to ensure that they are set up for the day, and can successfully go around their lessons learning, rather than begging for equipment from each teacher they come across.

With regard to equipment loan, there are two key issues, Monitoring, and stock. The latter is perhaps easier to solve. Ask your year leader (or if you are the year leader, ask your line manager) for a stock of equipment for each tutor group (pens, pencils, rubbers, rulers, calculators, etc.). Then, tutors will then have everything that they need to support their tutees at the start of the day. The thing to consider will be the monitoring.

Does your school have consequences for missing equipment? If it doesn't, should it? Consider how you are going to record missing equipment (signatures in a diary/planner, perhaps)? Equally, how will a tutor keep a track of loans? A recommendation here would be a clipboard with names of tutees, columns for different equipment, where a date is inserted where students borrow the equipment. Simply check each morning to see what equipment your tutees need to return to you from the previous day?

Behaviour Conversations

With tutor time often sitting at the beginning or end of the day, it provides a fantastic opportunity to speak to students about their behaviour. If you have students coming to you at the start of the day, then you can set them up to get things right, or if you have students at the end of the day, it will allow you to reflect on behaviours shown and celebrate what can be celebrated, and work on areas of concern and consider what needs to go better the next day.

By doing this, behaviour conversations can be had much sooner than, for example, waiting for a head of year to come and follow up with a student. Equally, we know that dealing with behaviour as soon as possible is the best way forward, otherwise behaviours and feelings can be forgotten. Speaking to a student about some bad lessons from several days ago is not going to be a productive conversation, as they will likely have forgotten what happened.

Speaking to a tutor, rather than a head of year or other member of staff also has two other major benefits. The first is that, over time, it would be hoped that a tutor would develop very strong, and positive ties with their tutees. With most tutors overseeing a group of students from Year 7 upwards, the tutor will be able to develop an understanding of what makes their tutees tick, and their strengths and areas for social and personal development. Therefore, it would be hoped that a student would be more open and honest in a conversation with their tutor. Second, where tutors lead on these conversations it adds another level of intervention. If middle or senior leaders were to lead on conversations for all behaviour, including fairly low-level behaviour (that does need to be challenged, but perhaps is not, comparatively, that 'bad'), there are two issues. The first is workload – these leaders will never get around to see all of the students they need to. Second is with regard to escalation. If only a head of year speaks to students about behaviour, the next escalation would be up to senior leadership. By adding in tutors at the bottom, it provides you with greater wiggle room when it comes to escalation.

In terms of the data that is analysed to lead these conversations, consider the following:

- The number of consequences that a student is receiving
- If they are the same subject/teacher
- If there is a particular period
- If a particular period follows a period of unstructured time
- If there are common students in lessons of concern
- If there are particular days

There are other factors that you can consider, but identifying any of these trends will give you the basis for a highly informative, and hopefully transformational conversation with your tutee.

Attendance Conversations

In very much the same way that a tutor can lead on conversations with tutees regarding behaviour, they can also lead on conversations with regard to attendance, for many of the same reasons as given above.

Though most, if not all schools have an attendance officer, it again cannot only be their responsibility to follow up on attendance issues. Once more, attendance officers only have raw data in front of them on most occasions, and do not have the reasons for absence, beyond a coding, for why students were off.

This is where tutors come in. Are there patterns that are developing with student absence, or perhaps there is a recurring illness, such as tonsillitis, that students are reasonably struggling with, and is not reflected by the 'Ill' code that they receive on the register?

Tutors will also be able to establish other patterns that the attendance officer or team may not be able to. For example, tutors may notice that there are certain days that students are missing, which may be down to lessons that they have, such as outdoor PE lessons where they have to change, or other reasons, such as a Friday or Monday off to work, as can be the case with some students.

Furthermore, tutors are often in a better position to speak to students with regard to attendance, due to that positive relationship that they have with tutees. When a member of the attendance team challenges a student, it is often only for 'bad' reasons. If a tutor has a conversation, they can have this from a place of confidence, trust and knowledge of the student, which will hopefully ensure that the conversations can go well.

Finally, once more, if tutors lead on these conversations in the first instance, there again is room for escalation up the school, for example to the attendance officer and later the SLT, should attendance not improve. It would also be wise to ensure that tutors have a way to pass on any crucial information that they glean from students, for example transport issues or taking a sibling to school first, especially in scenarios where the school may be able to put interventions into place to support.

SLT Drop-ins

There will be times, unfortunately, where SLT do need to speak to students. This could be due to a large number of varying reasons, but typically will come back to poor behaviour and attendance. There are two issues that senior leadership will often face, though. That is, when do they actually have the time to have these conversations, and second, how can they have these conversations without pulling students out of lessons and thus disrupting learning time?

Fortunately, tutor time provides the answers to both of these questions. First, SLT are very unlikely (and typically shouldn't, in an ideal world) have a tutor group. This therefore frees up a time where the SLT members are free where they may not otherwise be. In addition to this, taking students out of tutor time typically provides an opportunity to reduce the impact of removing a student from a class. There are of course concerns around missing out on workshops, tutor conversations, messages and a tutor programme, but this will typically be less impactful than pulling students out of lessons.

If SLT pops into tutor time on a regular basis too, this also will help improve standards of behaviour. It is common for behaviour in a group to improve when someone pops in, especially leadership, so this will also occur during tutor time. Equally, it provides SLT with an opportunity to see students in a different, typically non-academic lesson scenario, have more relaxed and informal conversations, and catch students doing the right things. This provides a brilliant opportunity to improve teacher-student relationships, rather than only meeting students when you're having to have tough conversations around behaviour, or attendance, for example.

Mobile Phone Conversations

Mobile phones are such a big topic in schools, aren't they? Should students be allowed to have them, or not? If they are allowed phones in school, are they allowed to use them? If not, are phones being placed into pockets sufficient? Should phones be handed in at reception? Or is there a full ban on phones coming onto the premises?

Once again, that is not a debate for this book to have – every school will already have their own policy regarding mobile phones which needs to be enforced. A tutor time provides a good opportunity to speak to students around the rules regarding phones, and why these rules have been introduced, as well as the consequences for breaking any rules.

Maximising Tutor Time

It provides an opportunity to have quieter, one-to-one conversations with students if they have broken mobile phone rules. For example, it would be possible for a tutor to speak to a student regarding the consequences they have already faced, and escalation were it to happen again. Tutor time, where it is held at the end of the day, also provides an opportunity for any confiscated mobile phones to be returned to students. In some schools, tutors may already have them ready to return, or they may be held centrally by a head of year/pastoral team or a school office.

However, if you are sending students off to collect phones during a tutor time, do consider the number of students on corridors, whether they can just collect a phone at the end of the day, and whether students will just start checking their phone for notifications as soon as they collect it.

Head of Year Interventions

A Head of Year (HoY) is constantly going to have students whom they are wanting to work with. Perhaps there are concerns around their academic progress, or possibly their out-of-lesson behaviour, or maybe even truancy whilst at school. A HoY will know their cohort better than anyone in school, and they are definitely the people to go to in order to identify the key groups of students.

Though a pastoral system does not *rely* upon a HoY, a lot of the work, especially around interventions, does fall onto them. For example, where tutors can monitor behaviour reports/contracts, and perhaps a member of the SLT can monitor attendance and persistent absenteeism, a HoY really is the one to get students into issues around lateness, out-of-lesson behaviour and slipping academic progress. And the best way to deal with this? Interventions!

The issue that a HoY has is time. When do they hold these interventions? They can't hold them during the day as students will be in lessons.

Break and lunch isn't fair on the students or the teacher, and afterschool really just is not a go-er. That leaves tutor time.

So long as tutors know what they need to be doing, there is the scope for a HoY to be busy, for at least one tutor period per week, in order to run an intervention. Even better, if a HoY has a second or deputy, they would also be able to hold an intervention. (However, I'd recommend that these were on separate days if at all possible, to ensure that at least one of the pastoral members for a year group is available during a tutor period).

I would recommend here that interventions take place over the course of a half-term. Any less time than that, and any impact will be limited or non-existent. Any longer than that, and a HoY (or their second) simply will not see that many different students in interventions across the year. Sometimes this may be necessary, if a group of students are needing more than 6 or 7 weeks worth of input, but ideally, working with six different sets of students, on six different sets of issues across the course of the year, would be ideal.

What interventions could a HoY run? Below are some ideas of interventions that could be run, if you do not already have them, or equivalent, running in your schools!

- Reasons for lateness
- Improving organisation
- Making homework and revision plans
- Exploring in-lesson poor behaviour
- Exploring out-of-lesson poor behaviour
- Considering reasons for non-attendance and how to address them
- Subject specific interventions (normally in-keeping with the HoYs specialist subject).

One recommendation I have here is that these interventions are placed onto the timetable of whoever is running them. This will help to ensure that they are not pulled for cover (as HoY are so often pulled to cover a tutor off work). Equally, I'd recommend booking a consistent room for the weeks of the intervention. Students will know exactly where they are going (no excuses for walking around the school site) and it also means that you don't spend half of your allotted time walking around trying to find an empty space or room to actually run your intervention!

Also, make notes about what works well, and what doesn't. This means that the next time you run that, or a similar intervention, you can ensure that it is even better than the last time, maximising the impact that the time with those students will have.

Pick Up Students for Detention

Often, tutor time will be held before a break in the day – whether that be a morning break, lunch break, or the end of the day. Usually, as well, schools will have detentions on some, or all of those times in the day.

Now, although we would love students to naturally make their way to a detention at a break, lunch, or afterschool, we also know that this may not always happen. Sometimes a student may genuinely forget (though if they have already been informed by their tutor, and especially if the detention is straight away after the tutor period, this a poor excuse). We also know, however, that there are more than enough students who will decide simply not to turn up to a detention.

Some schools may naturally consequence this – perhaps by escalating the consequence (a break detention becomes a lunch one; a lunch detention becomes an after-school one and so on). However, for some schools, there is not the capacity to do this, so if students are booked in for detention at any given time, they really need to be there.

Therefore, tutor time, where it sits before one of these detention times, provides the opportunity to go around and collect all students who need to be in there. This ensures there is no genuine forgetting, or otherwise, of the detention by students.

This is particularly helpful when a tutor period is held just before the end of the day, as then students can be collected 5 minutes before the end and taken to wherever the after-school detention is being held. This is typically the detention slot, in my experience, that students are so eager to miss, because it stops them getting home on time and being able to travel back with friends.

One consideration against this suggestion is whether students become too reliant on you collecting them (what happens if you are off one day and they are not collected)? Also, ought students take responsibility for getting to their detention rather than being 'dragged' there? Additionally, though this takes some pressure off a tutor to remind students about detention (there will be plenty of things to distract them), may this method lull tutors into a false sense of security meaning that they never inform students? A couple of counter points there to consider when deciding if this is the best policy for your students and school.

Pick Up Students for Isolation

Much like the previous suggestion, but this time focusing on where a tutor period is held before the start of the day, this time allows for all students who are going to be in isolation for the day to be collected and taken to the required location.

Often it can be hard to communicate to tutors which students are in isolation for the day, unless many emails get sent out. Therefore, going to collect the students during a morning tutor time (or at the end of it before they enter circulation for lessons for the day) ensures that all students who are supposed to be in isolation are there from the beginning.

It also means that any issues that stem from a student believing that they should not be in isolation for the day (perhaps they believe it is unfair or they haven't done something that they have been accused of) can be dealt with during a tutor time, rather than in the middle of a teaching lesson. It also provides students with some time to calm down and prepare themselves for a day in isolation, rather than entering 'hot headed', which would not be the ideal start (and could well trigger other students in the room).

Furthermore, sometimes students may genuinely not know that they are supposed to be in isolation. Going to collect these students from their first teaching lesson of the day can be time-consuming, but also extremely disruptive to the lessons that are going on. By collecting all students during a morning tutor time, you will be able to prevent this from happening in the first instance. A win win!

Setting and Checking Contracts

Behaviour is always one of the key areas for the pastoral, and hence tutor team, to be working on. This suggestion doesn't focus on who ought to be going on a contract, but focuses on how this can be successfully implemented by a tutor during tutor time.

First, it should be noted that the words contract, report, target card, etc., are all used interchangeably, and though all different in their own ways, are all focusing in on key behaviours that we would want to see from students (usually framing the behaviours we *do not* want to see, but in a positive spin!).

Contracts are hard enough to complete for a teacher at the end of a lesson – but monitoring and following up on them is a completely different, and more substantial, matter. For this to be done properly, time needs to be allocated in a tutor programme for tutors to monitor the contract process.

1. Speak to students to identify what areas that they think they need to work on.
2. Compare with data (e.g. is the student correct that it is subject x, y and z where issues normally occur)?
3. Develop 3 (ish!) targets for the contract, written with a positive framing (no more talking becomes silent until asked to talk, for example).
4. Agree check in times (will this be every tutor period, every other, end of the school day, every lunch? I would recommend every tutor period as this is allocated pastoral time).
5. Agree what success looks like.
6. Contact home regarding the contract, and inform members of staff of the contract.
7. Monitor report.
8. Monitoring conversations and taking students off the contract.

For a contract to be successful, there are lots of key stages which need to be completed fully. Ensure, therefore, that you allocate tutors the time to actually do this.

Some other top tips for ensuring that this is a success:

- Agree a contract format and provide digital or physical copies for all tutors.
- Agree a contract process – perhaps the eight steps above or something more context specific.
- Agree who makes contact home and with teachers (tutors or HoY?).
- Ensure that all contract targets are written in the same way.
- Ensure that consequences for 'failing' a contract are the same between tutors (for example, one tutor cannot give detentions for a 'failed' day if another just says 'do better tomorrow').

- Ensure consistency between year groups so that teachers know each contract that they are completing is the same type. There is nothing more frustrating for a classroom teacher than multiple different contracts all being completed in different ways!

Clear Message Communication

One of the biggest issues with student messaging is its inconsistencies. This isn't the fault of tutors either – messages get given in one way, interpreted, and then given out to students. Tutors will interpret things in different ways, place emphasis on different parts of messages or potentially even miss out features that they don't think are important. This is human nature!

The best way I have ever seen messages given out is through a standardised format that is shown or delivered in exactly the same way to students by all of the tutors within that year group. This can be done in two different ways.

The first way is by the HoY, or whoever it is who provides the notices for that day, collating them all on an email that is sent out to all tutors. Tutors then either display the text from this email, or tutors read it out word for word. This ensures that there are no issues around message interpretation, and also nothing missed when passing the message on to the tutor in the first instance either! For this method to work, however, the format ought to be similar day in day out, and should come from one source. If several people are emailing about notices to be given to students, it does get very confusing, especially where these notices are all given in different formats!

The other way I have seen this done successfully is where notices are embedded into a standard PowerPoint slide that is already up on the board when tutees enter their tutor period. Once again, this is a consistent approach in getting messages across to students and is not down to the interpretation of a tutor or tutee. Moreover, it reduces workload for a tutor, especially where they need to do a register, uniform checks, send students to intervention, get to an assembly, etc., as they can simply place this straight up on the board! Though it does take a little time for whomever is in charge of this daily slide to produce and share it, once a common template that is liked is found, it becomes a second nature part of the routine which is helpful for all.

Homework Follow-up

One of the biggest bug-bears in schools is homework completion – or rather, the lack of homework completion! Tutor time offers a dual opportunity – a chance to get ahead on revision and homework, if you so wish, or a chance to get organised and follow up on any homework concerns.

So first, you may decide that, if you have a lengthier tutor time period, and especially if it is at the end of the day, it may be a good chance for students to get started with homework, especially if there is computer access at school, where there may not be for a student at home. This is a great way to set a culture that homework must be done, but also that it is additional work, and not punishment, so if you can get some of it done whilst in school, then go for it! Of course, doing 'homework' in school does slightly defeat the purpose of homeworking, but it still gives students the opportunity to do extra work, revision and cementing new learning from the day. It also provides students with the opportunity to collaborate and support each other, which they may not be able to do at home. Also, depending on the subject specialty of the tutor, there may be the opportunity for students to get some support with their homework, too. In fact, I have also encouraged students to do homework that they have which is the same as the subject specialty of their tutor, because then they can ask for help if they need.

You may decide not to go down this route – often because there isn't enough time to do homework, or enough days in the week to dedicate a tutor session to completing homework. Instead, you may decide to focus on homework follow-up. This could involve the following:

- Placing students on a homework report
- Monitoring a homework report
- Sorting access issues for homework
- Helping students to prioritise key pieces of homework
- Having one-to-one conversations with students around their homework completion and any barriers that they may face
- Discussing ideal homework completion conditions (e.g. quiet, warm room, not too hot, and water available!)

My suggestion here would be to focus on homework contracts, if this is something that your school has (or wants to introduce), and then having conversations with students with regard to why homework is not being completed. I would suggest that tutors need to be provided with the data informing them which students have the worst homework completion rates, and in which subjects. Though there are many homework logging systems in use across schools, it isn't fair for tutors to have to click through 30 individual student profiles to see who is, and who isn't, completing homework, and in which subjects there are the most issues. These conversations of course, may lead on to some of the other bullet points above, such as how to prioritise work and ideal conditions to complete homework tasks in.

Sorting Out IT Issues

The final 'messaging' strategy! And it is quite the 'adminy' one – sorting out IT issues. Schools are entirely swamped (and dependent) on technology now. Homework tasks are often logged through an online portal (even if students do still have paper diaries and are encouraged to write down homework tasks in there, as well). Beyond this, lots of homework tasks are now set with online platforms, especially for Maths and the sciences. In summary, the vast majority of homework is on online platforms which require logins.

Much of the time, these platforms will all use a central login. But sometimes, they don't. And this is what leads to students not being able to login, not being able to reset passwords, and not being able to access and subsequently complete homework.

I would recommend that teachers are all provided with a master sheet of what login details look like for each of the different platforms that students need to have access to (e.g. is it joebloggs, jbloggs, and jbloggs25), as well as instructions on how to reset passwords, or who they need to go to in order to sort login details. It is all good and well asking tutors to support with IT access, but if they themselves don't understand or use the platforms, then they aren't going to be very much help at all!

By providing a central sheet with all of these instructions, you ensure that all students are getting the same clear, factually correct and concise information that they need. Also, once done, the document will never need to be re-done (unless platforms change or new ones are purchased). Additionally, it ensures that if tutors identify, in their homework one-to-one conversations, that logins are an issue for homework, then they are able to sort that then and there, rather than needing to refer the student on to another member of staff.

2 Events of the Year

Within school, there are a number of different key event days. Some of these are local, some national, and some international. One problem we often have is that they creep up on us too fast! It may mean that they get missed, or engagement with the events is not as significant as it could be, as planning time is too limited.

The aim of this chapter is to gather together information on all of these key event days, to allow for you to consider which are most relevant for you to include within your school day, as well as your tutor programme. This chapter also considers how you can engage with these events, and moves beyond just 'doing an assembly'.

This chapter ends with a calendar of the key events, for your planning ease! The aim, therefore, of this chapter, is to ensure that you have successfully planned in engagement with all of the key local, national and international events of the year.

Black History Month

Black History Month is something that has now become more commonplace across both schools, and society more generally, which is fantastic. However, far too often, Black History Month is left to the history department to lead on, or individual members of staff

 DOI: 10.4324/9781003605881-3

who have the desire to lead on it. But it should not be like this! The best way to get it cemented into the school calendar? By getting it into your tutor programme! This also means that the workload of any activities, assemblies and so forth, can be spread around the staff body, rather than just a few individuals.

The month itself is an opportunity to celebrate the contributions of black people to the country we now have, as well as raising awareness of prejudices and injustices that black people have, and continue to face, both in the United Kingdom, and worldwide. It's a government backed campaign too, meaning that there is plenty of press coverage and hence many resources are made afresh for schools each year. So, before you begin your Black History Month planning, take some time to have a look at what new resources are available.

So, what could you do in order to support Black History Month and raise awareness for your students?

- Get tutor groups to research individuals from the black community who have made significant contributions to society or specific areas of knowledge. Tutor groups could choose their own individuals or be given individuals to research.
- Produce a display based upon all of the individuals who are researched and place it in a well seen area within the school. Ensure that this gets updated each year too, so that it isn't static.
- Join in any competitions that are being run, perhaps around storytelling or poetry.
- Research black individuals who have been leaders around the world, and consider the barriers that they faced to reach their positions.
- Get students to produce a report, poster or some type of informative document on a black idol of their choosing.
- Choose and watch several of the BBC produced videos for Black History Month. Consider whether there are specific videos that support your curriculum too, in order to support subject cross-over.

Maximising Tutor Time

- Watch Horrible History episodes which cover black history.
- Produce lists of inventions which have come about due to the genius of black inventors.
- Another fairly common option – produce an assembly that can be delivered to all years within a school. This could be done by the history department or specific members of staff who do want to lead on it, or developed and delivered by a, or several, tutor groups.
- Explore literary documents which tell us something of black history, such as poetry to do with the Windrush scandal.
- Consider key organisations in the advancement of black rights. How have they gone about delivering improved rights? What organisations still exist, why, and what are their aims?
- Consider the black history of your local area. Rather than focusing on international or even national development, consider what happened, and is happening, in *your* area.
- Listen to music by black artists, who are both in the mainstream now, and previously.

Remembrance Day

Remembrance Day, observed on November 11th each year, is one of the staples of the school calendar. Two things are almost certainly going to happen – a 2-minute silence observed either on the 11th or the Friday before a weekend (where the 11th falls on a weekend), as well as a school assembly, explaining the significance of the day, as well as providing some information about the Great War, and those lost in them.

However, there is far more that you can do in order to commemorate Remembrance Day, including:

- Getting students (certain tutor groups or a year group) to design a display to go on a corridor board somewhere prominent, or in reception, in advance of remembrance.

- Ensure that poppies are sold in school, with students possibly going around to sell them, perhaps during a tutor time.
- Engaging with poetry from the war, such as 'In Flanders Field' by John McCrae, and discussing this during tutor time, including reflecting on the purpose of the poetry and trying to understand how it would have been for people living during those times.
- Listen to songs that relate to remembrance, such as the "Last Post", and again discuss with students the lyrics of certain songs, or how the songs make them feel.
- Get students (again, certain tutor groups or a year group) to actually research, plan and then deliver the school wide assembly for remembrance.
- Get students (as above) to produce a video that can be shared with the community about why remembrance is so important.
- Get students to speak to family and friends about any relatives or connections that they have with people in the war, and find a format to share these (as part of an audio recording, perhaps?)
- Identify key pieces of art from the period, and consider how they demonstrate the sacrifices of men and women from the time.
- Consider the big changes that occurred in society following World War One.
- Read a book in tutor time that relates to the War.
- Conduct a virtual visit to a war memorial.

Anti-Bullying Week

Rather than just a day of raising awareness, the anti-bullying campaign runs over the course of a week, often towards the end of the calendar year. In previous years, a mark of anti-bullying week has been to wear odd socks on one day to help to raise awareness. Bullying is of course a huge issue in schools – any school which says it has no bullying is ignorant to what goes on when teachers cannot see or hear. There is always more to do with regards to tackling bullying, and anti-bullying week is a great opportunity to raise awareness, challenge attitudes and weed out the behaviours that we do not want to be seeing our young people display (and to encourage the behaviours that we *do* want to be seeing).

So, what could you do to raise awareness of anti-bullying week, but more important, help to tackle bullying, during tutor time?

- Watch the BBC Teach lesson that has been produced specific-ally for Anti-Bullying week. This is a great resource that could be watched over a couple of tutor time sessions.
- Get tutees to research organisations that are, or have engaged, with anti-bullying organisations and events, such as the Premier League.
- Find out what the Anti-Bullying Week campaign is doing that year, e.g. odd socks, and encourage your tutees to engage with the campaign.
- Get tutor groups to develop an assembly, or to deliver the Anti-Bullying Week assembly on bullying to their own year group.
- Get tutor groups to develop a tutor group pledge on what they will do to stop, or tackle any bullying that they see.
- Get students to make their own pledges on what they can do in order to tackle bullying.
- Ensure that the school council conducts a survey around bullying to inform their discussions and feedback to the Senior Leadership Team.
- Get tutees to go around the school selling Anti-Bullying Week merchandise.
- Deliver the specifically tailored Anti-Bullying Week lessons over the course of a week of tutor periods.
- Discuss with students what makes something banter, and what makes something bullying.
- Identify, within the tutor group or between tutors, what the main bullying issues are in your context and establish plans to tackle them.

- Consider whether you could become a 'United Against Bullying School'.
- Get students to develop resources that can be handed out to parents and guardians.

One crucial thing to discuss before you deliver any of these strategies are ground rules. Students need to understand what they can, and cannot say. Students also ought to be continuously signposted to members of staff that they can speak to if anything upsets them during the week, or if they wish to make a disclosure regarding any bullying they may have seen or been on the receiving end of.

Children in Need

Children in Need is one of the most iconic fundraising days. I'm sure that everyone has taken part in, helped to fundraise for, or donated money to some sort of Children in Need cause at some point! It is of course something which is done far more in primary schools than secondary schools, and something that seems to be lessening in schools now, due to the financial situations many of our students' families face. However, this doesn't mean that Children in Need is something that should no longer be in your tutor time programme. Just the opposite, in fact. There is plenty to discuss and do in tutor time!

Firstly, fundraising. This is the common thing that is done in schools around the country. What are some of the obvious, and less obvious things, that you can do, in order to raise funds?

- Bake sale.
- Non-uniform day.
- Join in with the national challenges for Children in Need for your year!
- Get involved with the school specific challenges set.

- Join in with any physical challenges being set, which are often completed at a certain time in the day.
- Organise a bring and buy or a raffle.
- Get students to do sponsored challenges.
- Run challenges, such as a spelling bee.
- Get teachers to do horrific challenges, such as a teacher disco, head shave or baked bean bath!
- Reading challenges (another great cross-curricular link!).
- Sponsored silence (and I'm sure that there are many students we can think of whom we'd love to include in this!).

Now, beyond fundraising, there are many other things that you can do. These ideas include:

- The most obvious one is getting students to actually plan and run the fundraising activities that are mentioned above. In the weeks, and months, running up to the day, can students decide what they want to do? Can each tutor group be responsible for one activity that they plan and run completely? The 'soft' skills being developed here are huge!
- Get your tutor group to research into any local projects that have come about due to Children in Need funding. Can a display be produced somewhere in school to display all of this information? Could it be collated into a letter or article that could get sent home to parents and guardians or maybe put into the local newspaper?
- Watch the Children in Need films, available on their website online, suitable for students, to understand the issues that exist in the UK, and why their fundraising is so important.
- Challenge students to produce a history of Children in Need. When was it formed? Why? What does the future look like for Children in Need? Are there fundraising targets? How do they determine these?

- For deeper discussions – go into depth on why we need events like Children in Need, and what fundamentally needs to change so that fundraising days like them, no longer need to happen.

World AIDS Day

A further international day that we are probably all aware of is World AIDS Day, which is typically held on 1st December. It is nice to have an event in December which isn't just focusing on Christmas and Christmas celebrations, and allows us to focus on other worthy causes.

The purpose of World AIDS Day is to raise awareness of AIDS, and to show support for those who live with AIDS, and those who have sadly lost their lives. Though AIDS is a disease which can be ended, it is a cause that is being held back by poor management, a lack of funding, and a lack of awareness. This, therefore, is what this 'World Day', supported by the UN, is looking to focus on.

Now before you head straight on into supporting World AIDS Day, we need to remember that there is often stigma around the issues, as well as a significant number of misconceptions. Therefore, this may be the first point you want to tackle during a tutor time on the day, perhaps using resources provided annually by the World AIDS Day schools and colleges website. It would be a brilliant way to spend a tutor time, helping to educate students on such an important area. So, besides having an informative student presentation, quiz or talk, what else could you do?

- Sell or freely distribute red ribbons, which are available from the World AIDS Day school and college website (at the time of publishing!).
- Utilise other resources from the World AIDS Day school and college website, which at the time of writing include murder mystery packs, quizzes, escape and whodunnit events. A plethora

of resources which are different from those included for other world or national days, allowing this day, and these events to be clearly different during your tutor programme.

- Get students to display information posters around school.
- Consider fundraising activities that you can organise with your tutor groups (but there may be priority on other events, such as Children in Need, which is mentioned next).
- Utilise the lesson plans provided by the National AIDS Trust teachers website, allowing you to deliver factually correct and hard-hitting mini-lessons on AIDS.
- Get science tutor led forms to research, plan and deliver mini-lessons, assemblies, or produce recordings, with regards to AIDS and the science behind it (cross-curricular links!).
- Get history tutor led forms to research, plan and deliver mini lessons, assemblies, or produce recordings, with regards to AIDS and the history behind drug development and stigma behind it (cross-curricular links!).
- Develop social media posts in tutor groups that could go out through a school's social media channels (once they've been double checked, of course!).

Safer Internet Day

Safer Internet Day is hosted each year, typically around February, and raises focus on the dangers of the internet, how to stay safe online, and how to ensure that young people enjoy the internet in an appropriate fashion. This day is part of a worldwide movement for safer internet use, so there are also often worldwide events, competitions and organisations that you can join in with as well.

So, what can you do to get involved with Safer Internet Day?

- Consider how this can be tied in with your PSE curriculum. At some point, students will need to cover how to use the internet, risks that are posed and so forth. Is it possible to tie this in and complete activities during a tutor time?

- Identify key videos to watch with students and discuss what is shown.
- Choose resources from the Safer Internet Day campaign website to utilise during tutor time.
- Encourage tutors to join in with webinars by the Safer Internet Day team so that they can find out more about the dangers of the internet and how best to support students.
- Discuss reputable websites, and what a scam or untrustworthy source may look like.
- Make parents/guardians aware of the day so that they can speak to their students about it.
- Get students to research around Safer Internet Day and produce resources for younger years, and possibly to share with parents/guardians.
- Consider getting a tutor group to produce and present an assembly on the risks and dangers of the internet and how to stay safe, which they deliver to all other year groups.

St Andrews/St Davids/St George and St Patrick's Day

These national days are perhaps the most obvious, because they are ones most commonly celebrated in the general community, and not specific to schools, or younger individuals. All of the nations of the United Kingdom have their own specific saint, and celebrating these days is a wonderful way of connecting with heritage, history and developing a sense of culture amongst students and the school community. Equally, there is no reason why students in all parts of the UK shouldn't know and study the national days of the other UK nations, so even if the saint isn't *yours, consider* whether you can still raise awareness in your own school!

Maximising Tutor Time

What could you do then, to celebrate these days?

- Allow students to come in in national dress/wearing national symbols as part of the day.
- Get students to research their saint and to develop a presentation that they share with their tutor or year group.
- Split students in your tutor group into four, and give them each a saint to research. They can then teach each other about the different saints – four birds, one stone!
- Consider if there is the chance for an assembly – something that is fun and celebrates these days.
- Research traditional songs that students could listen to on the day. Do you have a choir – could they perform some of these songs? (You could use tutor periods in the run up to your national day to do all of the rehearsals).
- Produce a poem which celebrates the national saint.
- Challenge students to debate the importance of these national days, and whether they should be consigned to history, or whether they are still important.
- Consider if there is any origami that you can produce relevant to your saint or national day.
- Design, or compete in a national quiz. How much do your students know about the country that you live in? Could you make this competitive by splitting the tutor group into teams?
- Is there a special national food for your national day? Could students bake and bring these in to share on the day?
- Research how national symbols became so – for example, the daffodil for Wales and St David's day!
- Learn some native tongue – Welsh or Gaelic, for example!
- Research to find out if there are any parades that you can join with your tutor group or direct your students to outside of school hours.

World Refugee Day

World Refugee Day is organised and pushed forward by the United Nations – designed to build empathy and understanding for the plight of refugees across the world. It is often celebrated just before the end of the school term in summer, and sometimes can coincide with a week's worth of events. This is one of the more international events on this list, as well as a pertinent issue following crises in the Middle East, such as in Syria and Afghanistan.

So, what could you be doing in school to educate students and to raise awareness?

- Begin by using the UN website to understand the key terms used in discussing refugees, including stateless person, migration and displacement.
- Show students videos produced by the UNHCR for the year that you are raising awareness of this issue (so that students get the most up-to-date videos!).
- Get students to find three reasons why there is a need for World Refugee Day (the UN and UNHCR websites are very good places to look).
- See if there are any fundraising activities that you can get involved with, as a tutor group during a tutor period, in relation to any current conflicts or crises'.
- As a tutor group, design 'simple acts' that they, or the community could do, to support the refugee crisis.
- Consider whether your school could become a 'School of Sanctuary'.
- Develop an 'anti-racism' charter with your tutor group.
- Develop a day of welcoming where you ensure that all students in your school who are refugees are made to feel welcome, supported and celebrated.

- Explore the history of refugees – where the term was first coined, how it has developed, and the international laws to support refugees.
- Join in with any Q&A sessions which are organised to support the day.
- Research into celebrities and sports people who are refugees.

Pride Month

Much like Black History Month, pride celebrations, whether over the course of a week or a month have become far more commonplace across schools. Once more, these celebrations provide an opportunity to raise awareness of oppression that the LGBTQ community has faced, as well as a chance to celebrate some very famous LGBTQ individuals who have made some wonderful and significant contributions to society. So, what can you do during your tutor programme to support this?

- Find students or tutor groups who are happy to put together an informative assembly on pride and the LGBTQ community that they can share with the school.
- For a more hard-hitting conversation, discuss terms that people may use for members of the LGBTQ community which are highly offensive and shouldn't be used. If you do decide to do this, there will need to be clearly agreed and defined ground rules that all staff and students follow. However, it offers a great opportunity to discuss words that students may believe are fine to use, when in reality, they really are not!
- Discuss TV shows and films that centre around the LGBTQ community. What have students watched? What have they enjoyed?
- Separately, can students discuss TV shows and films that they have enjoyed where the main actor or actors are themselves part of the LGBTQ community?

- Get students to research the meaning behind the rainbow flag, as well as the origin of pride celebrations. When did they begin? What were their aims? What persecution have people faced?
- Utilise Stonewall resources. These often get updated each year, so see what is available the year that you are hosting and/or organising events.
- Provide students with a list of inspiring LGBTQ books.
- Consider tutor-based reading focusing on one of these LGBTQ books (as above).
- Consider famous LGBTQ sportspeople and the difficulties that they face. Could a discussion be held on trans rights for example? Or perhaps a conversation could be had on why so few footballers have come out as members of the LGBTQ community.
- Could a tutor time be used as an opportunity to start an LGBTQ student group? Could they research how LGBTQ students feel within school? Could they have representation on a school council? Lots of things to consider!

Student Idols

One very underrated area to focus on is students identifying their own idols. I've often seen this done as part of transition work, typically for students moving from a primary school aged 11 up to the big scary world of secondary school. However, it actually provides a super task to give to students in all year groups.

With regards to how it works – it's simple. Determine a format that you want students to communicate their idol – whether that is through a short presentation, a written report, a poster, and then let them get to work. This task shouldn't require computers in the main – or at least not for much of the research – and should be possible within one or two tutor sessions, depending on how long your sessions extend for.

Maximising Tutor Time

The benefits for this are many. Firstly, students get to communicate someone that they look up to. It's nice for students to get the opportunity to talk about individuals that may not often be talked about, especially because there are often some incredible anecdotes behind why these individuals are so inspirational. Building from this, as a tutor, you get to learn so much about your tutees, through understanding who they look up to – through who they idolise. This is a wonderful way to help build a relationship with students, especially where there is common ground between who they look up to, and who you also look up to.

Furthermore, this is a great chance for students to improve their communication skills – in whatever format(s) you have determined – on a topic that they themselves are passionate about. Of course, we cannot (always) create a curriculum around what students enjoy and are passionate about, but activities like this do allow for students to have some individuality and express their own passions. It's certainly no bad thing!

School Specific Celebrations

At some point in each school's history, you're likely to have had a 'famous' person go through – someone who has become famous – hopefully, for all of the right reasons! For many schools, this is someone to celebrate, someone to find out more about and challenge students to be as 'great' as that individual was. Sometimes, it may not actually have been a student who has walked through the school gates who is inspiring, but someone that the school is linked to. Perhaps it's a saint, or it is someone who opened the building, grew up on the same street or so forth. Whatever it may be, each school is likely to have at least one of these 'famous' or 'well known' individuals whom it is fun to celebrate and educate your students on.

This is a great opportunity to celebrate your school's history and culture. You could try and invite this individual in – once a year would be a great opportunity to keep these connections strong and inspire your students. Perhaps they could work with a tutor group in each year group, who could then share what they did with the other tutor groups within their year group? Or maybe they work with tutor groups in one year group each time they come in, so that all students are exposed to their school's 'person' once during their school career.

It may also be an opportunity to get the local community involved, especially if your school specific celebrations are in relation to an important community member, or something that your community is known for. Perhaps you could have a coffee morning organised by a tutor group, or get tutor groups to produce displays for local community halls and so forth.

Calendar of Events

Black History Month – October

Remembrance Day – 11 November

St Andrews Day – 30 November

Anit-Bullying Week – November

Children in Need – November

World AIDS Day – December

Safer Internet Day – February

St Davids Day – 1 March

St Patricks Day – 17 March

St Georges Day – 23 April

World Refugee Day – 20 June

Pride Month – June

3   Creativity Section

With the often restrictive nature of GCSE curricula, as well as the quantity of work that has to be completed within Key Stage 3, the opportunity for students to be creative is often limited. This is understandable. Knowledge has to come first, and in fact, knowledge is actually the underpinning requisite of creativity.

However, without providing opportunities for students to be creative – to think outside the box, apply their knowledge in different ways, and to push the (academic) boundaries – we are limited their all-round development as a young student. It would be easy to tell faculty areas to build in creativity to their curricula, but there just is not the time and space.

Therefore, the aim of this chapter is to provide you with a number of different ways that creativity can be included, and carefully scaffolded, within a wider tutor time curriculum.

Poem of the Day

Poetry offers a great opportunity for student creativity and language exploration, as well as ensuring cross-curricular coordination between departments and tutor time. As referred to many times within this book so far, and many more times to come too, there

 DOI: 10.4324/9781003605881-4

just is not the opportunity to cover all content within lesson time, so where tutor periods can support this, as well as developing more cultural capital opportunities for students, the better.

Though named 'poem of the day' the suggestion here is not that you would do a poem every single day – this would take up far too much time to deliver, and more time to plan than would be available. Instead, why not have a poem every fortnight, within a dedicated 'creativity' part of your tutor timetable? Within that part of the time-table, you would be able to cover many of the following creative suggestions! With regards to planning, this is something that you would likely want to draw on the support of the English faculty. Are there specific poems that would work well to support curriculum content? Or do they want students engaging with a wide range of different poetry even if it is not linked to the curriculum? You may also want to look at links with other curriculum areas – possible MFL or History, where poetry could be explored with reference to periods of time that students are studying. Ideally, you would want your faculty partners to give you a set of poems for the year so that you are not having to chase them up through the weeks.

Running this could lead to some pushback – are all teachers going to be happy delivering mini poetry sessions? I would argue that they would not be – so avoid this! Why not just have a poem that is read to, or by the students, and then some follow up questions that students could make notes about, discuss with the person next to them, or answer to the class. You do not need to have big follow up discussions and significant impact – the benefit of this top tutor time tip is simply exposing students to more poetry than they other-wise would be!

Additionally, if you are lucky, you may come across some poetry competitions that you can enter. Therefore, you may want to change this poem of the day to a mini poetry section where students are able to produce their own poems to submit to competition. Once again, there is not going to be the expert teacher support, but if doing this in a tutor time means students get to enter competitions that they would not otherwise be able to enter due to curriculum time constraints, then this has to be a bonus! And even if there are no competitions to enter, perhaps the English faculty could run one at the end of each academic year, with students drawing upon their exposure to new poems throughout the year during tutor time?

Word of the Day

Word of the day focuses on language development and exposure in much the same way as the previous idea – but is a little more focused in helping to develop the vocabulary of students – never a bad thing!

Once again, this is probably not an activity to do every single day, but maybe once or twice a week. You would again want faculty support, but depending on the way that you want to take this top tip, you do not necessarily have to just focus on the English faculty. If you simply want to broaden students' vocabulary knowledge, then yes, perhaps you do want all of these keywords to be provided to you by the English faculty. However, this top tip provides a brilliant opportunity to develop subject specific vocabulary. Why can't each key faculty provide words that they want students to be completely aware of? These may even vary by year, too. For example, Maths may want students to be clear on the word parallel in year 7, but by year 11, students need to understand words such as congruent or proof. By taking key words from a range of different faculties, you are reducing the workload for any one individual or faculty, and you are also ensuring that there is tutor time support for all faculties within your school.

An unexpected benefit here is a little bit of staff development. There are certain words from a curriculum perspective that staff may not be aware of, and so actually becoming aware of them through this top tip would be beneficial too! If all individuals can be learning together, this is a good thing. I think it is always good too for students to see their teachers delivering and discussing other subjects with them.

This idea, more so than the previous, would also be hugely beneficial in supporting any literacy and oratory plans that your school has, or will be putting in place; it is a superb way to support cross-school language development!

Thought for the Day

This top tip opens up the opportunity for some fantastic conversations in tutor time – and at a time when students are so addicted to phones and social media, an opportunity to get students conversing nicely should not be passed up.

The idea here is to provide students with a challenging quote. It could be someone's favourite quote, in relation to the day it is (e.g. a national day), a religious text or something hugely thought provoking. Whatever it may be, this quote ought to challenge the thinking of students, generate discussion and generate conversation.

Logistically, there are different ways of going about this depending on how collaborative your school environment is and the expectations placed on staff to support the tutor programme. One nice way of doing this is getting every member of staff to provide a quote that they like. This could be done anonymously, or when given to students, they could be told that it is *teacher x's* favourite quote, and maybe why. If you decide not to go down this route, you instead could get different year leaders to provide a few quotes, or again farm it out to different departments to get quotes that are relevant to their subject areas. Again, the sooner that you can get a bank of quotes for the year ahead, the better, otherwise you will end up chasing people.

Maximising Tutor Time

When delivering the thought for the day, there are a few different ways to go about it. You could possibly get students to read out the thought, or read it out yourself as the form tutor. Then, different pointer questions could be used to question students with, or to generate conversations in pairs, groups or as a whole class discussion. Example prompts could include:

- How will you change your actions today because of this thought?
- Are there any examples in your life which link to this thought for the day?
- Why do you think it is important that we consider this topic?
- Do you know the person who delivered this quote or thought? What are they famous for? Why were they important?

There are so many ways that you can take this top tip and run with it – all generating great thinking and some superb conversation!

Prayer for the Day

This is a top tip more in line for religious schools around the country. Though you will likely already be having a prayer in school each day, is tutor time a good opportunity to deliver the prayer, and allow for discussion after it? For example, if you have a prayer time before lunch or the end of the day, does it get rushed because people want to get off? Or maybe there is not the chance to discuss the prayer and what it means because people are wanting to get off?

If you do have prayers in school, you will likely already have one person who collates them, or a text that you get them from. If not, then this is probably your first step! You also need to ensure that these prayers are relevant to your students and school community, and if they are displayed, for example in a presentation, that they are clear and legible.

To extend the prayer time, you could provide students with some statements or questions that they need to consider, or even respond to. These could include:

- How are you going to change your actions today?
- Is there anything that you need to pray for?
- Are there things in your life that you need to reconsider?

Reflections of course can be private and personal, so it may not be relevant for students to share them. However, having a common opportunity for prayer and reflection, especially in silence, is the perfect thing to have during a tutor time. Moreover, this is something that you could have every single day – possible straight after the register at the beginning of tutor time? This gives you the maximum time to explore anything and everything that you and your students may want to, and ensures that the prayer is not rushed at the end of your tutor period!

Religious Passage for the Day

Following on from the previous suggestion, and again especially true for faith schools (but not limited too, as this provides a cross-curricular opportunity otherwise), is the exploration of religious texts, for example from the Bible. This is an expansion on just delivering a prayer to students during tutor time, and instead gives you 'more meat on the bones' to consider, and will allow for greater depth to reflections and discussions.

Depending on the faith of your school, readings may link in with your religious calendar – for example Christian schools will reflect on readings around the birth of Jesus during Advent. Again, you will be the experts in your own schools, so will know which texts will tie in best with your religious calendar. However, if you decide not to go down this route (or maybe there is not always necessarily a religious event to link with), different, but poignant readings can be selected. Again, you will be in the best place to decide what is best for your students and your school community.

How you deliver these passages for the day will vary – again you may get students to read them (you may already have volunteers who support religious activities and readings in your school and take a lead on this) or you may deliver it as the tutor in the room. Again, follow up questions are good – but time will need to be taken to ensure that questions link well with both the passage that has been read, as well as with what students will be concerned about. There is nothing worse than students not being engaged with a passage and then having ill-fitting questions posed to them.

Depending on the length of your tutor period, this may be something that you are able to do each day – possible after or before you do the prayer for the day. If your tutor time is not that long, then maybe it can be done once a week? Either way, it will need to be tailored specifically to your community and students.

Famous People Born on this Day

This top tip, as well as those that follow, are simply brilliant ways to support students' cultural capital – something that we know can always do with boosting! Every day is a school day, and the more that we can get students to learn, especially of the society and culture around them, the better.

One way in which to do this is to reflect on famous people born on that day. There are multiple ways of doing this, with many websites listing them, or even just a quick search of your favourite web browser will pull up options for that day. This is then information that you could share with students, and the following could be questions to ask or points of conversation:

- Do we know any of these famous people? How?
- What did they do in their lives?

- How have they impacted our lives?
- Who is similar to this person in our country, or in the world more generally now?

You can even take this further by getting students to produce little information packs on people, especially if they come across some-body who really chimes in with their lives and what they believe. Furthermore, you could even flip this whole process. Instead of telling students about famous people born on that specific day, why not get students to find someone famous born on that day that they know and is relevant to them. Maybe it will be a footballer, an influencer or a more modern star. However, this is a great way to get students talking about someone who matters to them, and getting them to explain why this person is so important. This may seem like a 'dumbing down' of this tip, but is actually a really fantastic way to get students enthused about talking with regards to someone who they know or really care about.

Once again, this is something that you're unlikely to do every single day, but maybe once or twice a fortnight, as it should only be a quick 5-minute activity. If you wanted to take it a bit further though, tutor groups could be given a future date to research, and then produce a presentation or assembly on an important individual that they then share with other tutor groups in their year, or even the whole school, on that day in the future. How enthused can you get your students with these ideas?

Famous Events on this Day

Another fantastic day-to-day reflection to consider is famous events that happened on your current day. Once again, this is a very easy thing to do with numerous websites listing these or a simple web search likely to bring up lots of different ideas that can be discussed in class.

Once again, this is something that can lead on to questioning and a huge amount of discussion. Prompts, which could be used by the tutor for the whole class, or given over for group discussions, include:

- What do you know about this event?
- When did it happen? Where did it happen? What happened?
- Do you know anyone who was involved?
- How did it change the future?
- Does that event still impact us now? How?
- Are things going to change back to how they were before this event?

Again, not all of these prompts may be helpful, but they are a starting point.

A couple of points of consideration here, though. Firstly, the historical events that are likely to crop up can be quite heavy hitting, especially around wars and more modern terror attacks. Whether you delve into these, or have a look at other events, will be up to you and how your students will react to them. They provide great opportunities for discussion but require far more monitoring around comments and behaviours. This is certainly not a reason to avoid them, but something to consider. Secondly, it will also be worth considering the events that you are coming up with in tutor time and those being studied in other subjects, mainly history, but also elsewhere. Is there a way you can tie in your historical event of the day to something students are, will or have studied previously? If it is something that students have or are currently looking at, then this is hugely beneficial as it should mean greater responses to the prompts, provided above, and allow for better conversation, as well as a good opportunity for content recall by students as well. This could easily be coordinated with having a skim over the schemes of learning for other subjects, or getting your history teachers to point out which events you would like covered by this top tip.

Once again, it may be that you only do this once a week, or once a fortnight, even. It is, however, one of those things that may need to vary the day in which it is done on the timetable, to ensure that you are hitting those key historic events that you want to discuss. No points doing a 'what historic thing happened on this day' and then choosing something that happened 3 days prior!

General Knowledge Quizzes

The next two ideas are wonderful ways to break up some of the heavier content that may be covered during a tutor time, especially if you are cramming in lots of new learning, cross-curricular links and conversation around behaviours and routines. This top tip focuses on giving students the opportunity to complete a general knowledge quiz.

Often done off a tutors own back, students will already, I am sure, get the opportunity to complete a quiz here or there during their tutor periods, often in the run up to Christmas. However, why not make this a more common thing, that happens because it is in a tutor timetable rather than a tutor running it because they have spent the time finding or making one? This is a great opportunity to run a general knowledge quiz at the end of each term.

Why not turn it into a competition? There are many ways to do this – maybe by splitting a tutor group up into different teams, putting tutor groups within a year against each other, or even pitting year groups against each other (can those Year 7s surprise you?). Budgets are stretched, right now, but is there any money remaining in the pastoral budget for a few small prizes for the winning teams or tutor groups?

Doing quizzes appeases students – it is always something that they seem to be asking for! However, from a learning point of view, it is a great chance to test students on a range of different general knowledge content. Of course, you will need to ensure that most, if not all of the questions are actually answerable by your students – there is no point getting last night's University Challenge questions printed off! Equally, I would suggest avoiding curriculum content. Though it may seem like a good opportunity to test and revise some key content, the purpose of this tip is to get students enthused with something which is quite far removed from their normal school day and tutor time activity.

What Happened this Week? Quizzes

Much like the previous top tip – breaking up the tutor programme and the school day with a quiz – you can probably work out the emphasis with this idea – doing a quiz at the end of each week. Not only does this make a bit of a change for students, it will also hopefully make them more aware, or at least try to get them more aware of what is happening in the outside, 'real' world. That is the only way that they are going to be able to prepare for this quiz, and thrive at it.

It may take some time to actually see students changing attitudes to do well at this quiz, but hopefully you will get some students wanting to check the BBC news pages from time to time. Any sort of increased engagement with the news of the day will be of benefit to students, as far too often they will only see and hear as far as their social media connections allow them.

Once again, this tip may involve splitting your tutor group up into teams, or doing tutor group versus tutor groups, or even years versus years. However, I recommend splitting up tutor groups and allowing students to compete against each other. As this is some-thing that you will hopefully be doing every single week – I mean, it is in the name! – then it is something that you will be able to keep a leaderboard of and see which teams are winning. This is what will hopefully get students tuning in to the news, as there are no barriers to their success (for example, sets or 'ability' do not matter, but keeping up with world events does, and is the only ingredient to success). Again, if possible and within budget, some small prizes, maybe at the end of the term for the winning team or teams within each tutor group would be a great step forward. If it is not possible, potentially think about other non-financial rewards or how it can be tied in with your school policy around rewarding positive behaviours?

As stated, this is a once per week activity – and if you are going to commit to it becoming some type of competition, then you will need to ensure that it actually does happen every single week. A Friday often works, as you can review the week that has just gone. In terms of resourcing, mainly online news platforms, including the BBC (at the time of writing) produce a little summary quiz of the week just been, that is published on a Friday morning. This is a great way to ensure that you have got a high-quality resource to run this top tip without increasing your workload.

House Competitions

The final top tip in this section of creativity, and it links in with one of the other suggestions within this book, which is a house system. If you have a house system, or are considering introducing one, then it is crucial that you get the most out of it. One of the best ways to do that is through competition, and considering that this is the creative section of the book, here are some creative suggestions!

- Introducing a poetry competition. This will link it really nicely if you do introduce the 'poem of the day' top tip from the start of this section.
- Consider how you can make one of the quiz options a house quiz. Could each tutor group in a year nominate a quizzer to form a year group team? Or maybe one nominee from each tutor

group goes head-to-head with other tutor groups to earn their houses points?

- Consider artistic opportunities – especially those which link in with key prayers and thoughts for the day. Could competitions be run on how these could be displayed around the school?
- Taking this further, could some form of art competition, or exhibition even, be coordinated to show off students' artistic talents, whilst also focusing on the house side of things?
- Creativity comes in all shapes and sizes – so there are also opportunities and music, dance and drama which could be explored. This will vary on the hobbies that students have as well as the curricular, and extra-curricular offering, that your school has.

Now of course these competitions are not going to be run every single week. It may be that a whole week is given up to competitions, or one day every term to limit disruption. Ensure that you know how you are going to go about this well in advance – students and tutors will need to know. There is nothing worse than determining a new tutor timetable with copious numbers of interesting new activities for it all to get thrown up into the air for a few days with no warning because of house competitions.

4 The Brain and Learning

If we had three wishes, I often believe that I would use one of them to make my students more effective and efficient learners. How many times do we hear of students revising in ineffective ways? Or not taking on board feedback? Or not knowing where (or even when) to turn for further help?

However, students are not going to become better at revising, more effective learners, or more independent, without being taught how to do this. A lot of this can be done within the curriculum of our subject areas, yes, but it can also be supported through a high-quality tutor programme, which introduces students to ideas of cognitive science, allowing them to understand the why behind effective revision techniques, the importance of reflection, and what a good working environment is like, amongst many other things.

By the end of this chapter, you will have a number of different ideas as to how a strong tutor time curriculum can better prepare our students for the demands of secondary and post-16 education, by making them more effective and efficient learners, who actually know how to revise!

DOI: 10.4324/9781003605881-5

Metacognition Sessions

Metacognition is a hugely powerful tool and hopefully something that you come across before. Metacognition is the consistent evaluation from the beginning to the end of a task with regards to how it's going. It involves considering how to plan for a task, how to monitor a task when you're completing it, to ensure that you are still heading in the correct direction, and of course evaluation at the end of the task to make sure you've done what you needed to do and consider how you can improve next time. I like to think of metacognition as a little voice inside your head which is constantly guiding your actions to improve effectiveness and efficiency. In fact, metacognition is the most impactful intervention as researched by the EEF. There is nothing more impactful than metacognition, but yet it's not something that we do much in schools, let alone explaining to our students.

This book isn't going to be the place to go into huge depths about metacognition. In fact, I've previously written dozens of several articles and a couple of books about the theory itself. It's crucial when you're planning your tutor timetable that metacognition is something that you do build in. So, without going too much into the why, because that is explained elsewhere, let's think about how you would do this.

The first thing you need to consider is what the different metacognitive things that you want students to improve on are. This needs to come from the leadership team, who evaluate year groups, or maybe the whole school as one. It's not really going to work at a faculty level because tutor groups are often not organised by faculty. The areas to consider focusing on are: planning, monitoring and evaluation which make up one of the two 'metacognitive cycles'. You'll need to choose which of these areas to focus on – or at least which of the three areas to focus on first. Once you have, you then need to consider strategies…

Picking strategies can be difficult, but as mentioned, this isn't really the book to go into all of that. The focus when choosing strategies is ensuring that they link in with the curriculum content across a range of subjects. The worst thing you can do is pick a strategy that would work for perhaps only one or two different subjects. The focus when choosing these strategies is ensuring that whatever you teach the students, that they can then go and use them in a range of different subjects both in class and, ideally, at home.

If you're having a look at planning, for example, you might want to challenge students to use cognitive planning grids that focus on their knowledge of task, knowledge of strategies and knowledge of self. This is a great strategy to ensure that students really consider what they know about a task and about the content needed for a task before they jump straight in. Other planning options that you might wish to have a look at are more problem-solving type styles, which would be especially helpful for maths and sciences. This type of planning grid would really focus on when students have completed similar tasks and the range of strategies that have got available for them, and allow students to consider the relative strength and weaknesses of each strategy available to them.

If you're considering monitoring strategies to support students then you might consider something like a flow map. A flow map does what it says on the tin, in that students write down all of the stages they go through or should be going through, in order to complete a task successfully. This is an incredibly adaptable strategy and especially helpful for SEN students as well, so it really is one of those strategies that supports all students across all subjects.

If you're looking at evaluation strategies, you might want to get students started on something like a wrapper early on. If you're not familiar with a wrapper, these are documents which list all of the questions contained within a task or exam paper and provide students with an opportunity to evaluate why they lost marks.

They're a great way for getting students to realise that maybe they weren't reading the questions correctly, maybe they didn't revise enough or maybe they didn't put enough detail in their answers.

There are copious other strategies we could teach students as well – these are just some of those you might want to get started with!

How to Revise

We all know how important revision is. Teachers know it, students know it, parents and guardians know it. Even if we as teachers and school staff know about effective revision, and even if we're getting better at telling students what effective revision is, there's still more we can do. One of the very best ways of doing this is ensuring that students get regular input and practice with some of these revision strategies during the tutor program, beginning from Year 7. It might seem a little bit early to start discussing revision strategies but even students in Year 7 are going to need to know how to revise for end of topic tests, or larger assessments that they may have before setting going into Year 8, for example. Additionally, the soon that students become comfortable with a range of effective revision techniques the better.

So, before we dive into how you should go about organising this part of tutor time, we should consider some effective revision strategies that you want to be teaching to students. We know that note taking and highlighting isn't very effective, so we probably want to dissuade students from those techniques. Instead, we want students making flashcards. We want students doing self-testing. We want students completing past papers. We want students evaluating mark schemes and checking their answers against them. We want students to be trying to fill in gaps in knowledge organisers. We want students to interleave their learning as well.

Now you're ready to plan these sessions, what do you need to do? The first thing that you need to decide here is what effective revision techniques do you want students to learn? You need to ensure that the revision strategies chosen are ones that are actually helpful to the students in that year group. You also need to ensure that they are applicable strategies to the subjects and the content that you teach. Once you've done this, you're ready to plan your revision strategy tutor programme.

My suggestion would be that you double and triple check the strategies you are going to get tutors to deliver are the correct ones. Make sure that staff from different departments who teach different year groups are aware of the strategies before you start going to plan all of the sessions. By doing this you will ensure that staff buy into what you are doing and it will support the implementation of the sessions. Once you've done this double and triple checking you can then go and plan the sessions. You'll need to think carefully about which year groups are going to have the different revision strategies. The worst thing you can do is try to teach every year group every revision strategy. You simply won't have time to do this or at least not to do each strategy justice. There are also some strategies which just wouldn't be relevant for students further down the school or further up the school even.

The next recommendation is that you ensure that these are timetabled into the tutor programme, possibly one every month or every half term. This will help to ensure that the sessions are as equally spread out as possible. I'd also recommend that you keep a common format for all of the sessions, especially within a year group. This will benefit not only students who are trying to learn about these new strategies but also tutors who are going to have to deliver these sessions. The more consistency the better.

The next crucial thing is not just students learning about these strategies though – it's ensuring that they also practise them. Fortunately, that's where the next top tip comes in…

Revision Skills

There will be very little point teaching students about effective revision strategies if they never actually get to use them. This is where this top tip comes in. After you have delivered a new revision strategy to students, make sure that they then get the opportunity to practice using it. We all know that if we don't plan in some deliberate practice, it's often not going to happen. That means that if we're just telling students how to revise effectively but not giving them an opportunity to do that with supervision, it's probably not going to happen. So, in the weeks between delivering new revision strategies to students you'll also need a timetable for some opportunities for students to practise them.

Now for GCSE students this is quite easy because it will often just be covered in homework or revision for assessments and mocks, and final exams that they have. It might be slightly more difficult to find activities for other year groups if they don't have general revision that they need to be getting on with. This is where a little bit of planning can go a long way. The recommendation here is to speak to each of your different core subject areas and get appropriate tasks that students can use to practise their new revision strategy on. For example, if students have just learned how to self-test, then possibly from history you could get a set of dates and events that students could then flashcard and self-test themselves against during a tutor time. If students have just been shown how to use a mark scheme, then maybe maths could provide some sample questions and some mark schemes so students can identify the errors in the working, or possibly give the questions a go themselves and then self-mark.

Now of course tutor time is very busy so you're not going to have a chance to do this every single week. However, it's not something that needs to take up a whole tutor time – possibly just 10 or 15 minutes. Maybe try to build in two of these time slots after each new revision strategy to ensure that students do have a little bit of a chance to bed in their new strategy. If these strategies are well timetabled into your tutor timetable, then subject areas are going to be able to link in their subject content to the latest revision strategy that students have just been taught. This is another fantastic way to develop cross curricular links, but also ensure that students get the deliberate practice but they need for the new revision strategy.

Fingertip Facts

Fingertip facts are a great way of helping to ensure that students can recall crucial subject knowledge at the click of a finger. So, what do we even mean by fingertip facts? We mean the type of information that would be included in a knowledge organiser. This means key formulas, key dates, key techniques and key stages in processes – all of that crucial information that students need to be able to recall instantly to support their learning.

We are in the unfortunate situation where there isn't enough time in the school day to be able to cover everything that we need to. Homework can be used of course, but sometimes this can be quite hit or miss and return rates can be poor. It isn't something that we can rely upon. So of course, this is where tutor time can step up and help to support.

Most schools these days have knowledge organisers and a lot of schools use these knowledge organisers to actually inform homework. Why not build in a fingertip fact session once per every half term where students revise the key facts from a knowledge organiser?

Students can choose which knowledge organiser that they want to use and which facts that they want to learn, and they can also decide whether they want to do this on their own or with the person sitting next to them. If you are a school with knowledge organisers, it makes it even easier because tutors can be supplied with a handful of spare copies for the inevitable moment when a student says that they don't have their knowledge organiser with them!

This might seem like it's going to be quite a noisy session but positively it's a great way of cementing some of those self-testing strategies that you'll have been teaching students during your revision strategy tutor times as well.

How to Do Homework

The next two strategies are fairly similar. However, there are subtle differences which will hopefully become clear. The first focus is on supporting students in how to actually complete homework, from a content point of view.

How many students do we know say they don't complete homework because they don't know what to do? It's probably the most historic excuse used for not completing homework, and the one that's going to be used the most in the future too! It doesn't matter how well a student seems to have learnt something in the lesson and it doesn't matter how many times you've gone over it, students are always going to use that excuse! However, we need to try to build resilience and give students some strategies that they can use if they really are stuck at home.

In terms of strategies that we can teach students, the first one might be the use of a dictionary or a thesaurus – even if it's by using Google. This is a great strategy to help students when they're struggling with writing tasks.

The next strategy that we can teach students is using their knowledge organisers, if you have them in your school. I've often found that knowledge drivers are given to students but not really explained to them in terms of how they should be using them. By ensuring during a tutor time that students know how to use a knowledge driver, it will mean that students can use them at home to support their homework and their learning.

The next way we can support students is by giving them high-quality websites that they can turn to in order to support them with their homework. Initially these effective websites are going to have to come from departments, who feed them through to year leaders and tutors. However, once a list has been formed, tutors can continue to tell students about these different options, so that students can recall where they need to go if they are stuck.

Another appropriate strategy to support students will be getting them over to a homework club. Most schools have homework club before or after school, or maybe even at lunchtime. Directing students to a homework club is no bad thing and means that students can get a little bit more support than if they were using the other strategies.

The final strategy is the use of a book. And by book, I mean the exercise books that students should be using in each lesson and keeping clear concise and good notes and answers. Sometimes students don't understand the purpose for having an exercise book or for keeping hold of it. By teaching students how they can look back in their books at examples and questions that they've completed, and how this can help them with similar tasks during homework, is a very effective way of giving students another strategy to get work done at home.

How to Ensure Homework Gets Completed

The very subtle difference with this top tip is not about the content of homework tasks, but about the planning and the organisation of homework. This itself is split into two sections – that of when to get homework done, and the other of the type of environment which is best to get work completed in. This top tip will focus on the former area, rather than the latter, which will be covered later.

Maximising Tutor Time

What ought we do then to help students keep on top of their homework, and how do we teach them this during tutor time? The first will be around the use of homework recording platforms, including a homework diary, if students are still provided with them. If students are provided with them, are they actually using them? If you deem them important, then it is crucial that you actually follow up with students and make sure that they are using them. Equally, students need to know how to use homework diaries. Ought they write homework on the day it was given to them, or on the day that it is due? Which option is best may vary by student, but it is a conversation worth happening (and I personally would always go for the latter!). Additionally, students ought to record down how long their work is going to take them. There is no point writing that a homework is due on a given day if it is actually going to take 4 hours to complete – this is not something that you can do the night before! This is where using online homework platforms can be helpful – and one reason why schools have moved towards them. On these platforms, which I am sure we have all now come across, it is possible for class teachers to record down how long a homework task will take. Again, we can help to teach students to use this information to plan out how long they need to be giving themselves for homework tasks.

Additionally, it is worth speaking to students about their extra-curricular activities. If students know that they have extended netball practice on a Wednesday night, then they need to make sure that all Thursday homework tasks are done by Tuesday night at the latest. Additionally, if students know that they have a busy weekend – possibly going to see family or the like – then they need to take this into account.

There are many ways to support students with this during tutor time. You could discuss these factors with students through a guided PowerPoint presentation delivered by tutors, or you could take it slightly further by ensuring that students plan out a timetable to complete their homework that incorporates all of their extra-curricular activities. This is especially easy if you have a school homework timetable, where it is clear on which days different subjects are going to give out homework tasks, and their respective hand in dates. I'd also recommend getting students to consider their timetable and identify opportunities to speak to their class teacher between a homework being given out and it being due in, should they need help and support with it.

Over time, you will know which students fall behind on homework, and those who are good at getting themselves organised. This will allow you to focus on just a few students who you perhaps work most intensively with in completing their homework task planning.

Whatever you do, it is certainly not going to harm you students by considering, and making it explicit, that they ought to consider, plan, and allot time to completing all of their homework tasks.

Habit Forming

Habits are incredibly important things for our young people to develop, but so often, students develop the wrong ones. Poor behaviour in the corridor, shouting out rather than raising hands, or not completing homework.

However, there are habits that we would all like to see – and again, tutor time provides an opportunity to introduce and nurture new habits in our students. This is because tutor time is held every single day, and so these habits can be re-affirmed every single day, until they become part of a student's normal routine.

The habits that we get students to form will vary hugely by institution. What works in one school will not work in another, and so forth. In this section, we are looking at the brain and learning, so the habits that we are focusing on are those around effective learning processes. However, these need to be habits that can be actively introduced, practised and refined during a tutor time. There is no point telling students to form the habit of working at a desk at home, because there is nothing that we can do to reinforce that.

You will need to consider your school aims when you consider which habits to introduce. These are also likely to fluctuate by year group. However, some suggestions are provided below:

- Always put your hand up when you have an answer to a question or want to ask a question
- Get out a dairy and/or pencil case when you enter a classroom
- Ensure that you get key equipment out on a desk when you sit down
- Copy down key notes as provided by a teacher
- Sit in silence when a teacher is talking

These may be the perfect habits for your students and school, but equally, you may want other habits formed in your students. Whatever you decide, ensure that this is a habit which can be revisited every single tutor time. If it cannot be done, then it will not be a habit formed. Choose areas to focus on, and ensure that they can be revisited every single day! Also, do not try to introduce too many at once – perhaps focusing on just one new habit at a time. Plus, do not forget to go back and revisit these habits in future too, otherwise they could potentially fall away once again.

How Learning Happens

As teaching staff, we are well aware of how learning happens. We understand short-term memory, long-term memory and cognitive loads. However, students don't know this. But does it help students to learn curriculum content if they actually understand how learning happens? I think so!

How do you go about this without making it too complicated? Once again, how much depth you go into may vary depending on the school you work in, but in short, understanding short- and long-term memory alongside working memory, as well as how information gets into short-term memory, and how and why we need information to get into long-term memory would be a very good start.

I'd recommend getting one common presentation that can be delivered to all students. Is there a reason why Year 7 students should not get the same input as Year 11 students? It may be wisest here to delegate this task to a teacher, or teachers in your school who have done research or delivered training around how the brain works, memory and cognitive loads. This will ensure that their expertise, and ability to simplify these concepts, can shine through.

Once again, I would recommend that this is delivered to all students through a PowerPoint presentation delivered to all year groups by tutors, who will need the resources in advance to ensure that they are happy delivering them, and can get any support that they require. This should be delivered at the start of the year, and then revisited at different points in the year, perhaps once every term.

Another thing that you can do is give students little tests – recall challenges – on the different facets of learning after you have delivered this initial presentation. This will ensure that the theory of learning stays fresh in the heads of all students, and will also pro-vide you with the opportunity to cover this content to students who were absent on the day that the original presentation was delivered.

The Working Environment

The penultimate tip for this section is around teaching students about the ideal environment in which to complete work, both inside school, but mainly outside school when revising and completing homework tasks. Once again, this is an area where as teachers we are confident in our understanding of what makes the typical, ideal, learning environment. But once again, students often are not told, get told individually if they come and ask for help, or work out the way in which *they* think they learn best.

Much like the previous suggestion, this top tip suggests getting an expert, or several, in your school to produce a presentation that can be shared with students. Again, this ought to be delivered to all students, and follow ups completed to try to help students form these positive habits outside of school. It may also be something that you can share with parents, for example by emailing the presentation home or by providing a top tips sheet that can go home.

So, what sort of things ought you consider in this presentation for students?

- Ambient working temperature – not too hot and not too cold.
- Quiet – though sometimes background noise such as classical music can help (but lyrical music can provide a negative cognitive load).
- A set space to work – e.g. a study, where possible.
- Taking yourself out of the working area when you are done.
- Trying to split the working area from the sleeping area.
- Taking regular breaks and getting fresh air.
- Eating fruit and drinking water. Stimulants are not all that helpful!
- Trying to work on a desk or a table, if possible, rather than just knees.

Of course, everyone has their own way of going about things, and some students (and even we as adults) may have habits that we have formed which do not chime with these top tips, and may not get replaced, just because we have been told otherwise. However, without telling students (and their families), how they *ought* to be working, how would they ever know otherwise?

Silent Reading

The final top tip for this section is around silent reading. It perhaps is one of the more obvious top tips in this whole book, but still incredibly important that it is actively considered, especially as it is likely to make a significant impact on a tutor timetable.

Literacy is a huge focus across schools right now, with too many students having a low reading age, and a large portion of students not reading sufficiently. These are two huge battles that we are having to fight, and the easiest, and most obvious solution, is to do something during school time. However, this is not that simple – where do you find the time? English already has two GCSEs to cover, so there isn't time there. Once again, this is where tutor time can step up.

Very often, schools timetable a silent reading session once a week – which feels like a very positive move forward. However, it is crucial that this becomes a block of time which doesn't get disrupted by unexpected events – wherever this is possible. This means that the timetabled day for reading is protected if it can be. I can hear English departments rejoicing even as I write these words!

One of the biggest blocks to this happening is students having books – and suitable books at that. This is where having a school library, or at least a good selection of books in each tutor room, is very helpful. Of course, you cannot have swathes of students going out to the library during their silent reading time, so actually having a range of books ready in each room is a very good way to go. And if students aren't enjoying themselves, well hopefully it will spark them to go and get a book from the library that they do want to read! That is of course, if you are still fortunate enough to have a library in your school.

This silent reading also provides an opportunity for tutors to have one-to-one conversations with their students, such as those mentioned earlier with regards to behaviour and homework. It also

Maximising Tutor Time

gives tutors a chance to go through any data that they need to, and maybe even get a few emails sent off to parents with regards to any pastoral updates that they have. It must be noted of course, that if you have a very long tutor time block, then you may not want to sue a whole session for silent reading – perhaps just 15 or 20 minutes.

5 Interventions

All subject areas wish that they had more time to deliver the content, and all subject areas wish that they had the time to run interventions to support students further in that subject area. Making the day longer than 24 hours, however, is not something any of us have yet managed to do.

However, making time is something that we do have within our power, as this chapter will show. Through a range of innovative and time efficient strategies, this chapter will illuminate a number of different approaches that can be taken in a tutor time programme to provide opportunity for academic intervention, that otherwise was not there.

It should be noted here, too, that these strategies are designed to be embedded within the routines of a tutor time curriculum. Interventions are often the ad hoc type of activity that is shoe-horned into a tutor time, because that is the only time left within the school day. The strategies given below are designed in order to avoid just this issue.

Numeracy Intervention

The first main intervention that you could consider running is with regards to numeracy. This could include, but is not limited to: times

DOI: 10.4324/9781003605881-6

tables, telling the time, money questions, real-life percentages and problems, fractions and general sums. Application of mathematics is important here.

Numeracy is an intervention which can be run across the board. No students are going to do worse for having had more opportunities to practise their numeracy, even if they end up getting everything correct each week. More practice is never going to be a *bad* thing! Generally however, numeracy interventions are incredibly helpful at getting students to think about everyday maths, as well as increasing their speed, efficiency and accuracy when doing 'small' calculations – things that in a maths lesson need to be done quickly, accurately and without fuss. Therefore, improvements made outside lessons can really help to support progress made within lessons.

There are many ways to go about running a numeracy intervention, but the most popular that I have come across is Numeracy Ninjas – a short, timed set of questions, with full answers available for students to self-mark. It builds in difficulty and allows students to improve each session that they do it. I am sure that there are other top numeracy interventions you could do too – it is just this one I am most familiar with. I would recommend running this once per week, because otherwise you simply will not have time to fit everything else into your tutor timetable. You may in fact decide to run it once per fortnight, and alternate with an English intervention – as discussed in the next top tip!

However you go about running it, it is often only KS3 students who are majorly going to benefit from this. By the time you get to KS4 and GCSE students, the benefits are likely to reduce because the spread of attainment within a year group will be giant – and so running this at a tutor level where students are not in sets can become difficult. That does not mean it is impossible though, so if you do decide to run it in KS4, consider how all students of all attainment levels can benefit.

So, those English interventions...?

English Intervention

The second top tip is that of running an English language type intervention – which is often centred around reading as this is the easiest thing to do normally during a tutor time, with regards to planning and logistics. Reading has already been mentioned as a key top tip though – so how does this differ?

When silent reading was discussed earlier, this was with regards to students just reading a book of their own choosing from home or maybe the school library. The focus there was just on increasing the amount of reading that students are doing and ensuring that they have time during the school day to do this. The focus with this top tip is on development around a certain text. The way I have seen it run is where the English department will choose a different book for each year group – something that is age relevant and helpful to what they are teaching – and then this gets read in tutor time. It is crucial here that the text is helpful for what is being studied in the subject, as the aim, as with the numeracy intervention above, is to increase student skills outside of lessons, so that they can then make greater progress when they are sat in their English lessons.

There are a few ways you may wish to go about this, and often they are budget dependent. Do you have enough money to buy a copy of the book for each student to read during a tutor time, or do they need to share? In fact, do you actually just need to show it on the screen? Equally, are students going to be reading the book out loud, or is it all going to be teacher led? Again, there are options here, and many will depend on your school context and what your English department wants to happen. What is their policy on reading, and especially active reading within class? Go and speak to them (or in fact you may already be the person in your school who is responsible for this!). Once you have, you will be able to ensure that your reading intervention is run in line with the expectations, and best available learning science, of the English faculty.

Faculty Led Interventions

So far, these top tips have focused on whole year group interventions around numeracy and English. Sometimes though, it is important to focus on interventions for individual students. This again, is something that can be done during a tutor time – so long as you have the input from, and support of, all of your different faculties.

Take the following example. There are a group of eight students in Year 7 who are falling behind where they would be expected to be – for whatever reason. They are working hard – the issues are not to do with behaviour or attendance – they simply just need some more support. However, as time goes on, they are falling further and further behind because their gaps are just not being resolved. *How do you go about fixing this issue?* That's right – using tutor time!

This top tip suggests that once these students have been identified (and you can see why faculty support on this is needed – because they are the ones who will need to identify the students for you), they receive small group catch-up interventions during their tutor time. Working with the head of department, a year group leader will need to choose an appropriate teacher to lead on these sessions during a tutor time. Often, it is the head of department who does this, especially for KS4 interventions.

There is a problem here, I hear you ask! The member of staff who will go off to lead that intervention is almost certainly going to have a tutor group, so who is going to cover that tutor group? Some solutions:

- In some schools, heads of department – or at least those for Maths, English and Science – do not have a tutor group. If this is workable, this is a way of getting 5 days' worth of intervention completed without the need for any cover.
- If cover is needed, consider whether the year group leader could fill in on that day?

- Could members of the leadership team produce a rota so that they can backfill some of these tutor group covers?
- Can external cover be used for a tutor group where they are already in school?
- To avoid cover, could interventions be put on assembly days, so that once the tutor group has been registered and taken to the hall, the tutor is free to go and run their intervention?

So there are a few solutions to the problems of cover. You may even have some more possibilities as well. To begin with, this intervention may just be run in KS4 for a larger number of subjects, or across all years, but just for Maths, English and Science. However you decide to run it, departments are going to need to step up in order to identify the correct students for any interventions, ensure that contact home has been made, that students are told why they are getting this intervention, as well as ensuring that the sessions are thoroughly planned.

Done well, this top tip has the potential to really support the academic catch-up and achievement of a large number of students.

Additional GCSEs

Depending on how long and how frequent your tutor sessions are, they may potentially provide an opportunity for an additional GCSE to be run – staff dependent, of course! Schools run Triple Science at GCSE, but squeezing this extra work into the allotted curriculum time can be difficult. On top of this, schools like to provide other options too, including Further Maths – a great gateway between GCSE and A-Levels. With curriculum time so tight, how do you even fit these in?

Schools fortunate enough to have a longer tutor time can exploit this to run additional GCSEs like those outlined above. Is it possible to take one, or maybe even two tutor sessions in a week in order to run these additional GCSEs? It massively reduces the stress on curriculum time, especially for Triple Science, and provides a superb opportunity for highly achieving students to gain an extra qualification that they otherwise wouldn't get.

Planning here is less of a concern than cover. In the previous tip, some solutions to cover interventions were provided, but those are unlikely to be suitable for long-term cover where these extra GCSEs are being run. Instead, you really need to have the capacity for a teacher not to have a tutor group, so that they have the time to both plan and run these additional sessions. Remember, the extra workload for the teacher here with regards to planning, marking, assessment and so on. Often, it would be a head of department who would do this. Do you have this capacity? If still no, do you have any part-time members of staff who possibly cannot have a whole tutor group to themselves, but could do a group share, opening up their colleague to run the additional GSCE sessions?

This top tip may not be logistically possible at all, but it certainly offers up a huge number of benefits if anything is workable.

Enrichment

Building from the previous top tip, tutor periods offer a superb opportunity for enrichment – especially around additional qualifications and courses. However, not every student can go on and on and complete an additional GCSE – practically, this just could never happen in the current education scenario. There is however, nothing stopping all students from doing additional projects and mini courses.

There are a few benefits of doing this. Firstly, it provides students with an opportunity to study something that they really want to do that they possibly do not currently get the chance to have a look at in school. Secondly, the more learning that students do, the better things should go in their lessons, hopefully improving their overall attainment. Lastly, if students are gaining extra qualifications, this will put them ahead of other students – and of course we have to do the best for the students who are sat in front of us.

Enrichment can take a lot of forms, but this top tip suggests utilising programmes and opportunities that are already in existence. The first of those is OpenLearn, a platform providing hundreds of short courses, all made by the Open University. These courses cover a huge range of topics, vary in their difficulties and also their lengths. This means that there will be the right course for every single student in your school, regardless of their interests or the time that they have to commit to the course. There may of course be alternative platforms like this, but the Open University name is a very good one to have on a qualification for students. Additionally, the Open University is famed for its high-quality online courses – these will be no different. They can be completed at home, but consider the opportunity for an enrichment part of your tutor timetable – possibly just every half-term to get students logged in, selecting courses and tracking progress. Is there any way that you could incentivise this further? Could you utilise the school rewards system, provide vouchers or run competitions for qualifications completed? Either way, take a look at what is on offer and see what your students can get involved with!

The second main option is the Project Qualifications. Many people are aware of the EPQ – the Enhanced Project Qualification, but this is actually one of three levels of the project. Their requirements change, but in effect students have to run a self-guided project, and complete a full write up. The higher the level of the project qualification, the more strenuous the expectations and write up are, of course! Students undertaking this will need a staff mentor – almost like a supervisor at university – as they work their way through the project. Though this can be done outside of lesson time for both students and teachers (if they are happy) this does not necessarily seem fair. If there is the option for students and teachers to be able to do this during a tutor time, that is certainly a win. With regards to the logistics of these qualifications, they are again well renowned and run by a number of different exam boards. Check out their websites to find out more!

Careers Activities

Careers work has always been crucial in schools, with perhaps more focus on it now than ever before. But when do you fit it in? Should students have a lesson on careers each week? Can it fit in with PSHE delivery? Or perhaps you could utilise non-curriculum days, often known as Drop Down Days, where specialists can come into school to deliver careers sessions? But perhaps one overlooked option is whether it can be infrequently built into the tutor timetable – possibly once per half-term?

Careers look completely different in every school. Some schools have strong links to local businesses, some have links to national businesses, and some have fewer links. Some schools and areas have work experience, others do not. Some schools have careers leads on the Senior Leadership Team, whereas in some secondary's this position is held by an unpaid member of staff. Exactly how careers work in your school will impact how you deliver careers education through your tutor time programme.

Could it be that high-quality videos are shown once per half-term as selected by the career's coordinator? Perhaps those careers quizzes and extra curriculum logs could be completed during this time as well? Or if you are blessed with a longer tutor time, is there even the chance to get in your external speakers then? Doing this will ensure that limited curriculum time is not lost – which has to be a benefit. You may also consider whether it is possible to use an assembly to deliver some of these career's work or provide an opportunity for these external speakers.

This top tip may appear 'woolly', but this is due to the huge variance in provision across schools. Consider what it is you already offer, what you want to be able to offer, and thus how tutor periods can be a useful opportunity to provide a vehicle for this.

Computer Access

Mentioned elsewhere in the book is the difficulty that some students can face accessing computers, especially where they need to complete homework. Though your school may have computers available for students to use for just this reason before school, after school, or even in a break or a lunch, is this fair? Should a student have to give a break during a school day just to do homework, because they cannot do it at home?

One solution to this is by ensuring that all students have a semi-regular opportunity to use computers during the school day. This has two benefits. The first is that *all* students, regardless of how on top of their homework they are (or are not!) will have the chance to get more done during the school day, and also be supported in completing it and planning which things they need to do first. Homework is by its very nature work that needs to be done at home, but students sometimes will need support in determining priorities, what they need to do and so forth. The opportunity to do this in school with their form tutor will ensure that they get that little bit of input that they need. The other benefit of ensuring that all students have this semi-regular computer access is so that students who do not have a computer at home do not have to raise this in front of their school friends. Though there should be nothing wrong with doing this, you can understand why a lot of students would not want to do this.

Having semi-regular computer access for tutor groups in a year actually is not too hard to do. Ensure that you have a rota for the days that different tutor groups are going to be using a room, and stick to it! The only reason why you may wish to cancel this is if you have cover with a group for whatever reason. If one tutor group within a year group is permanently based within a computer room, you may also need to swap them out with whichever tutor group is using the computers that day, or, to minimise disruption for them, try to find them a permanent, non-computer room to be based in.

Homework Interventions

Homework has its own section earlier on in this book, especially where it focuses in on tracking homework completion, having difficult conversations with students around homework completion, and then training students on how to complete homework and the ideal working environment. Some schools will even use contracts or reports for students who are not keeping on top of all of their homework, with the tutor responsible for keeping on top of this.

However, if students are not keeping up with their homework, or if they 'fail' their contract, what then? This top tip suggests that you could try to run a homework intervention with students who fall into either of these two categories. This could be run by a teaching assistant possibly, a teacher who does not have a tutor group, or even a year leader. These sessions could focus in on a number of different things, including:

- Timetabling when students are going to be completing their homework.
- Ensuring that students have all of the equipment that they need in order to complete their homework.
- Contacting home to parents and carers with any plans put in place.
- An opportunity to just get heads down and work completed.
- Identify any SEN interventions that may be needed to support homework.

- Follow up on the importance of homework and the reasons why it is given.
- Look at breaking tasks down into smaller, manageable chunks.
- Determine whether students need to cut back on the amount of homework that they are doing and focus on just a few core subjects to begin with.

There are a vast number of things that you can utilise these sessions for, which are likely to vary based upon the students that you have in front of you. The way you run these sessions for one group of students is going to vary hugely with the next group of students that you have.

Mixed Year Group Support

This intervention top tip again focuses on supporting specific groups of students from a curriculum point of view, especially Maths, Science and English. This top tip looks to identify key students who are all at a similar point in their learning – whether this be high fliers who need support to push up to a grade 9, or students in Year 7 who are struggling to keep up with the curriculum being taught.

The tip here is to group together around a dozen students with a few older students – maybe three- who can then support these students with whatever work that they may be doing. In practice, this may see a bunch of GCSE Maths higher questions being given to a group of students, for example, who are then supported by Year 12 A-Level Maths students.

There are many benefits for running an intervention like this. So many in fact, here is a list of just some of them:

- Highly beneficial interventions can be run without the need for additional cover where tutors have to be used to run a session.

- Students often like, or even prefer, having other students explain the work to them, rather than a teacher.
- This intervention is often very helpful for highly attaining students but ensures that they get stretch and challenge without needing more teacher input.
- Provide older students with the challenge of having to explain work, and not just 'do it'.
- Provide students with the opportunity to 'volunteer', which is often required for sixth Form students as part of applications or awards, such as the Duke of Edinburgh Award.

All in all, this top tip provides the opportunity for further academic support without creating a dramatic requirement for cover or huge planning workloads for teachers either.

SEN Workshops

There is so much work that our brilliant Special Education Needs teams need to do in schools, but there simply are not the resources or the time on so many occasions. I have however, seen tutor times be used superbly well for the benefit of the SEN departments and students. Though this is just one top tip, there are several ways, listed below, that the SEN department can utilise a block in tutor time for much good.

Access Arrangements

An absolutely crucial part of any exam season includes students getting any access arrangements that they need. But when are these students actually going to learn how to use any access that they have been given? Students cannot just turn up for their first ever GCSE exam and suddenly have a scribe, an overlay or additional time having never utilised or considered this arrangement before. Having sessions for students to practise using their arrangement, or discuss how it will work and strategies to make the most of it – for example extra time or rest breaks – is incredibly useful for students. It also ensures that students do not waste the access they have – which is often in the form of a teaching assistant who acts as a reader or a scribe for them. If TAs are not actually utilised in those situations, they may as well be in a lesson somewhere else!

Assessments

So many students arrive at secondary school not having the funding that they ought to have to support them in being successful at school. A lot of the time, these funding applications require a huge amount of evidence and chunks of time that just are not available at other times in the day. Tutor time offers an opportunity to sit down with students, without having to remove them from lessons or forcing them to miss a break and/or a lunchtime, in order to sit down and discuss any applications (as required) and collect any evidence with them (as required). It then also provides the SEN team with a little block of time in which to get some of these applications completed and sent away.

Behaviour Plans

Students with SEN can, as like any non-SEN student, struggle with behaviour. Often, the behaviours displayed by SEN students vary due to the SEN that they have, and therefore, the responses that are required to these behaviours vary. In many schools, student specific behaviour plans are formulated alongside the student, so that they can be shared with class teachers, and even staff more widely, to ensure that behaviours can be dealt with in both a sensitive, but effective manner, for each student. Once again, the question arises as to when you can actually complete these plans without pulling students from lessons or losing breaks or lunches. Once more, it is not really fair to ask a tutor to try to compile something like this with a student during a tutor time. Not only may they not have the same expertise as someone in the SEN department, it is also not a private opportunity for a student to discuss concerns, behaviours and responses if they have 30 classmates sitting right behind them!

Lesson Access Plans

This suggestion builds upon the first and third, and looks at access arrangements and plans for within lessons. Once again, some SEN students are likely to require some level of adaptation or addition to thrive within lessons. This can range from where the individual sits in the room, to answering questions, handing out worksheets and breaks outside of a classroom. Once again, these responses are often collated on a document that can be shared with teaching staff, so that they are in the best position to support that student within their lessons. Tutor time offers that perfect opportunity to sit down with students to create these plans without the stress of falling behind if it were done during a lesson.

There are four options here for utilising tutor time to support SEN attainment within school, but there are probably far more that you will be able to think of, especially if you are involved with SEN in your school.

CREST

Though CREST could fit in as a top tip as part of the enrichment section, it is its own top tip due to the relative complexity of how it needs to be run – that is – by a science teacher rather than just any member of staff who may be free.

CREST is a national award with three levels at secondary – Bronze, Silver and Gold (think Duke of Edinburgh award). At each level, the complexity and requirements increase, as do the number of hours required to run the sessions. However, this national award is a great one for students to get, as they enthuse themselves into a range of different projects and experiments. It can be especially helpful in supporting progress through GCSEs and pushing students up to A-Level sciences as well.

Unlike with some of the other enrichment options, CREST does require a science teacher to run it. And not only that, but the teacher is also going to need the time to plan the sessions and complete all of the associated paperwork that comes with administering the programme. This is often run, therefore, as an afterschool club, which often staff are happy to do and students will happily stay for – I have never heard anything but positive reviews for this award before! However, if you are fortunate enough to have longer tutor periods, would it not be beneficial to complete at least some of the award during this time? This is especially helpful for students who are unable to stay after school, for example due to transportation issues.

Brilliant Club

Another hugely popular national scheme that you may have come across previously is the *Brilliant Club*. A UK charity, this group looks to get high-quality individuals, such as current PhD students into schools, to lead on a university-esque type project. Previously, you have been able to select from a range of potential projects that you think will best suit the students that you choose, and then the charity will ensure that you have the perfect individual to mentor students through the programme. Through the course of the programme students engage with high-quality literature, consider how to go about producing a university type essay, including referencing, and also acting upon feedback. Often, students get to celebrate the end of the course through a 'graduation' at their partner university.

Once again, there are probably different organisations that offer this, or something similar, or it may even be something that you try to offer to students through your current staffing body. Perhaps you could even run this through the careers team? It is a wonderful opportunity to stretch a group of students and begin to expose them to the world of university life and learning. Projects can vary to suit the interests of your students, and the students that you pick are the ones that you want. Of course, you may need some input from different departments on who is chosen, and you may even want to make it competitive and challenge students to perform highly and work hard in order to get in on this type of project.

Overall, it provides a superb chance to learn more about university, not only from an academic point of view, but also with regards to how university works. Challenging students to be critical, and thinking about reading widely around a subject to support their arguments and critiques is also a wonderful skill to develop early, and will certainly work wonders in the attainment of students who take part across a number of different subjects.

Running a programme like this is perfectly possible during a tutor time – or at least, beginning in a tutor time. If your tutor time is at the end of the day, could you, for example, begin the session during the tutor time and finish it off afterschool, meaning that students do not have to be at school incredibly late? Having it during school time ensures that no students are omitted due to circumstances outside their control outside school, such as transport or being a young carer, too. And finally, I have also never found a student who has done this type of project, or similar, who hasn't really enjoyed it!

Mentoring

You are likely to have come across mentoring in a professional perspective, and potentially with students together (like a buddy system, which is explored below), but have you ever come across student-staff mentoring?

This top tip is a wonderful way to link up students with an appropriate member of staff, helping to challenge them and push them on to succeed as well as they possibly can. It involves as many staff being involved as possible, and really needs to include the Senior Leadership Team as well, if it can. But all members of staff can be involved! Here are some of the things that can be considered:

- Consider linking up students with staff members who studied at university the subject that they want to study.
- Consider linking up students with staff members who currently do, or have done, a job that the student is interested in doing.
- Consider working with students 1–2–1 on how to revise and get themselves organised.
- Consider working with students 1–2–1 on behaviour and how to change around the way they are conducting themselves in school.
- Consider working with students 1–2–1 on mental health and ensuring that they thrive during stressful or pressurised times, including, but not exclusive to, exams.
- Consider working with students 1–2–1 around ideas of confidence, especially for those doing performance subjects.

There are a huge number of reasons to link staff up to students, and often they don't need to be for academic reasons either. Yes, you may match up the Head of History with the student who can get a high grade at GCSE History but is currently struggling, but equally you may want to match them up with someone else who could be a slightly better fit.

It is up to you when students meet with their mentor, but if many students are linked up with heads of department or Senior Leadership who do not have a tutor group, then a tutor session provides an apt opportunity to catch up and continue conversations. It may also be possible to have these types of catch-up conversations during an assembly, where a tutor can 'become free'. I am sure that there are ways that you can make this work – it is certainly worth trying!

Buddy-Up System

The buddy-up system is likely one that you have come across before, but again, it is another one that should not be forgotten, and is especially good to run in a tutor time where all students will be outside curriculum teaching time.

In a buddy system, a number of students, often from lower years are identified as potentially needing some more support. There can be a number of reasons for this, which include, but are not limited to:

- Challenging behaviour
- Concerns around attendance
- Academic progress – especially in certain subjects
- Wanting advice around options
- Needing stretch and challenge
- Support completing homework
- Support with how to revise and when to do it
- Mental health support

These are all areas that, as covered by the other tips in this book, can be addressed during tutor time. That does not mean that we cannot go further though – why can we not try to deal with it in a buddy situation as well? Once you have carefully selected students who need support in one (or maybe more) of these or other areas, you then need to choose students that you can rely on to support these students. Often these are sixth form students, or they can also be Year 11 students. Identify the skills that the senior buddy will have, and then group them up with their younger year student.

A few things to consider, though, for this to be successful. Firstly, ensure that the senior buddy is clued up on safeguarding and understands what they need to refer on, and to whom. It may even be worth having brief minutes after each session to make sure nothing is missed. If students are talking about areas such as mental health, it may also be worth the senior buddy having a little training or literature that they can go through together with their buddy. This ensures a consistent, strong and safe approach to maintain safe advice. You will also need to consider attendance – if the senior buddy is often not in school, they may end up 'letting down' their younger buddy. You will also want to consider supervision, and how you can support the senior buddy with the sessions if they are struggling, for example, through question prompts.

Though this may seem like quite a lot of work to set up in the first instance – and it is a fair amount – once it is working, there will be many, many more times students getting support than if you were trying to do all of this on your own! The initial hard work will certainly pay off.

6 Enrichment

Tutor time offers a wonderful chance to provide more enrichment opportunities for our students; opportunities that they may otherwise not have. With families facing growing financial pressures, the chance to engage in 'enriching' activity is often not as possible for some students as it is for others. Yet, we know that many of these opportunities can be life-defining for our young people. The opportunity to try out a new sport, go to the theatre, or do a short course that they may not otherwise be able to do can have significant positive impacts on a young person.

But time is tight in schools, and so is money. The chance to provide these opportunities is small, and feels like it is diminishing. However, there are ways that we can provide enriching opportunities for our students. This chapter will detail a number of different strategies that can be embedded within a curriculum, in order to provide students with these enriching opportunities.

Sports

Students will get to take part in a wide range of different sports through their compulsory PE lessons. Students may even try different sports outside school, or at least go to clubs and do some

DOI: 10.4324/9781003605881-7

of the most common ones, such as gymnastics, football and rugby. However, due to the nature of the PE curriculum, it is simply impossible for all students to have a go at a very wide range of different sports – there simply is not the time. However, there are a huge range of sports out there that could really capture the imagination of students, simply by having the chance to play it.

You can see where this is going… Can tutor time step up and try to provide this enrichment for students? For example, would it be possible for a whole year group to have a drop down from a tutor session to go and try out a new sport? If this were to happen six times across the year – that is once per half-term – then students will be exposed for the first time, or for one of the first times, to six new sports.

This is great enrichment – opening students' eyes to different sports that are out there. Sports which they may want to watch and hopefully go and play themselves. I'm sure that amongst your PE department you will find inspiration and enthusiasm for students getting to try out different sports. It may even be that you do 'common sports' such as hockey and cricket, which again may just not quite make the cut when the curriculum is being planned.

You're unlikely to want students to get changed for these sessions, so picking less sweaty sports may be beneficial! You're also unlikely to have much coaching time – these really will just be sessions to dip into quickly, so maybe choose some sports which are fairly easy to grasp, or which can be simplified for quick play. I am sure you will find some brilliant new sports for your students to try out!

Language Sessions

Alongside sports, languages are a great enrichment opportunity for students. Though students up and down the UK now have the opportunity to study a Modern Foreign Language (MFL), these are often one of French, Spanish or German. Very helpful languages, but sometimes not languages which enthuse students (often, I have found, because they are the mandatory options, rather than students purely disliking languages more generally!).

Do you have speakers of different languages in your schools? Does anyone speak Japanese? Urdu perhaps? Or maybe even some Welsh? Would these teachers be prepared to run fun little taster sessions that students could get involved in? Who does not like to learn a bit of a new language? It is always good fun to pick up some new words or phrases in a language that you do not often hear!

It may also be that you have links to local Universities, and they may run little language taster sessions too. They may even offer to run language courses for your students outside school – maybe even as an additional GCSE. These are great avenues to explore, because you can get real experts in, and you avoid putting additional workload on any of your staff.

Logistically, you may want a whole year group to come together in the hall for example, to ensure that limited tutor time for a whole year group is impacted. You may, to improve participation from students, want to run this tutor group by tutor group across the course a single week – in the style of a standard lesson.

This again probably is not something that you do all of the time – although if you do have a lot of teachers who speak additional languages and are willing to share, then maybe you will. However, even if you just offer one or two of these sessions across a whole year, then a new and exciting opportunity is being offered to students. Who knows, you may find the thing that makes them fall in love with languages!

Music Lessons

The next opportunity for enrichment is a very well-known one – music! Learning to play a musical instrument is a wonderful thing – but often can be very expensive to do so. Procuring an instrument and then paying for lessons is prohibitive for a lot of people. Equally, actually listening to live music, such as the piano, is not that common either. How many opportunities do our young people have to actually just get to sit and listen to live piano music being played right in front of them? Probably not very many. So, what are the different ways that we can improve the musical enrichment of students in our schools? Here are just a handful of ideas:

- Are there any grants that you can get to support access to music lessons for your students?
- Are there any local charities or community groups who may be able to come in and provide some lessons free of charge to students?
- Are there any local charities who donate old instruments to students who want to learn to play?
- Are there any school funds to allow for students to earn a school scholarship to learn, or improve their playing?
- Are there any local charities or organisations who can come into school and offer taster music sessions to students – perhaps singing or learning an instrument?
- Can music lessons be organised so that they are in a tutor period, thus ensuring students do not miss lesson time?
- Are there any local musicians who may be happy coming in to play live music for students?
- Are there local musical offerings or carnivals where students can go out to and listen to live music to be inspired!

Depending on your locality, you may know of other things that are on offer, or may be available, to provide musical enrichment for your students. You will also know what your budgets look like. It may even be that you get your school orchestra and school choir to come and perform at several different assemblies throughout the year. This is great practice for those respective groups – both honing their skill and getting familiar with performing in front of larger crowds – especially difficult when they know everyone is looking back at them. It also provides a further opportunity for students to actually hear live music and catch the bug.

If students do catch the bug, do try and have places that you can direct students to. There is nothing worse than a student coming to say that they want to learn to play instrument x or y and then you not knowing where to direct them – that spark could quickly die away. The more opportunities that you can channel towards students, the better!

Green Activities

Another superb enrichment activity that students can get involved with, both within school and in their local area, are green activities. These types of activities may include local community initiatives, initiatives being pushed to schools by the Department for Education, or even more national charity led schemes.

We all know that the changing environment presents challenges and concerns, and so making students aware of this is hugely important, ensuring that they are aware of the world around them. Getting students involved in positive (but politically neutral) activities is a great way to take this further and support the enrichment of students. If students do get involved with local projects and schemes, not only are they doing some real good, but they are also working at something that they will later be able to put on their CV and talk about at interviews.

Finding the right programme for your school and students may take a little digging. I have previously seen schemes run by local charities for teenagers to create an item or service that would have a positive environmental impact in their local area. Teams of teens worked on this, with charity support, over the course of several months, before pitching their idea to the charity, alongside all of the other groups, at the end. The winning group then received the finances required to take their scheme/item and get it up and running.

Projects will of course vary, but this type of opportunity is a no-brainer to join in with. There will certainly be students keen on environmental issues in your school and this is a great way of providing them with real-life experience. Furthermore, a project of this type can be run during tutor time. If it runs once per week, and you have a timetabled 'enrichment' tutor time, this offers the perfect opportunity for students to go and complete any projects like this. Even if you cannot find any local charities or organisations running a project like this at your point in time, could you set up the equivalent school project (probably without the money at the end, mind)? It will still offer a great enrichment opportunity for students to practise teamwork, planning and presenting, amongst many other skills.

Newsletters

A superb enrichment opportunity for students is to get them engaged with the school newsletter. Many schools have run with a monthly or termly newsletter for many years, but after COVID, the number of schools who seem to do this seems to have grown exponentially.

The issue with newsletters is the amount of work that needs to go into them. Different departments need to do write-ups, school trips need to be documented, up-coming events need to be trailed. Sometimes putting this additional workload on staff can be difficult. Often there just is not the time, and where there is, it can be quite hard to get the brain focused on writing something fun and engaging after marking 100 past papers!

Maximising Tutor Time

But getting students involved in the newsletter has so many wonderful benefits. So many in fact, a list is required:

- Opportunity for students to practise their longer writing.
- Get student perspectives in the newsletters, rather than just the thoughts of teachers and staff.
- An increased quantity of articles as there are more potential student writers than staff writers.
- Provide an outlet for any budding authors and reporters.
- Provide students with something that they can record on their CV or talk about in future interviews.
- Give students an outlet for them to write about a topic that they really love and care about.
- Get a greater range of topics covered due to the greater range of student interests and hobbies.
- Support the English curriculum through the opportunity to write newsletter articles.
- Reduce staff workload (as hinted at above!).

You can get students to write about a huge number of topics. Again, there are so many, we need another list:

- What they are learning in their different subjects.
- Updates from the student leadership team.
- Updates from the student council.
- Reports 'from the playground'
- Events, from the perspective of students, such as open evenings or options events.
- Updates from school trips.
- Aims and excitement for future trips and opportunities.
- Reflections on school achievements.
- Writing about important days in the school calendar.
- Write-ups on local school sporting fixtures.
- Updates on school clubs and any performances, e.g. choir.

As you can see, getting students involved with the newsletter is a great opportunity for the students, and provides the opportunity for a very interesting newsletter! And it would not take too much time to do this either! You would maybe need to take one tutor period to split up who is writing about what, and then a further tutor period to get all of the write-ups completed. And if you are doing this each half-term, two tutor periods for a handful of students does not seem like too much of a commitment!

Allotment

The final top tip for this section is that of an allotment. Allotments have been around for a long time now, with many schools having an area either currently, or historically used as an allotment. The condition it is in, however, may be questionable! This though, provides a fantastic opportunity to tap into the green fingers of students. Getting them involved with an allotment is a wonderful opportunity to spark a life-long love of the outdoors and growing your own.

What are these benefits?

- Students get time in the fresh air, which can often be far too limited for far too many students.
- Students get to learn how to grow their own.
- Students can see the real-time growth of a plant and link it with their curriculum learning.
- Students can get inspired to complete gardening in the future.
- Students are exposed to a potential future career option.
- The allotment may be able to provide some food for the kitchens or cooking lessons.
- Students can take pride in their work from little seeds to fruit and veg that they can actually eat.
- Students can use this as a volunteering opportunity for a future CV, or programmes such as the Duke of Edinburgh's award.

- Students may get passionate enough that they apply for an allotment in their local area.
- A healthy allotment will make the school look a far nicer place.
- An opportunity for tranquillity and calm.
- A potential time-out space for some students who need it.
- Supporting local wildlife.

The great thing about allotments is, at a school level, they will often be free or very inexpensive to run. There are always schemes available for schools to get hold of bulbs and seeds for free or next to nothing, which you should definitely take advantage of. Local garden centres will often be happy to support this type of project too, whilst funds raised by groups such as the PTA can often be put towards this scheme. You may even just be able to ask for contributions from families – either financial or in terms of resources (people have often got seeds, plant pots and part bags of compost lying about that they wouldn't mind in the slightest getting rid of!).

This is something that may need to run a little more seasonally, and of course you do have the issue of what to do with the allotment over the summer. Do you have students, parents and some staff who may be happy to pop down once a week during those summer holidays just to keep an eye on everything (with the reward being the fruit and veg that is ready to pick?). Again, if you schedule an enrichment time to your timetable, getting a dozen or so students down onto the allotment for 30 minutes a week means that a huge amount of work can be done!

7 Current Affairs

It is sometimes argued that schools do not prepare students for the 'real-world'. Whether this is true or not is beyond the scope of this book, but one thing is true. Ensuring that our students do have an understanding of the 'real-world' is certainly a positive thing. Contributing to a better understanding of their context, as well as providing topics for discussion, and developing a more rounded individual, keeping up to date with current affairs is something very beneficial for our young people.

Going about this can be difficult. Current affairs are often very heavy, such as general election campaigns, or very upsetting, such as wars with ravage with hostility world-wide. But our students still need to know what is happening, but in a way that is suitable for their age group.

This chapter will explore a number of different ways that students can keep up to date with current affairs, whilst ensuring that activities are age-appropriate and suitable for our young people.

Watch Newsround

The first top tip is a simple one – simply show students Newsround! If we want students to become engaged and knowledgeable about the

DOI: 10.4324/9781003605881-8

world around them, the easiest way to do this is simply by watching the news. However, the normal, for example, 10 O'Clock news, is both too long and probably a little bit too heavy hitting for many teenagers. It's a common adult thing to say that everything we see on the news is sad and depressing, so this is probably not the way that we want to either start, or end the day with our tutees in a tutor time.

Newsround, though, is a specially designed news show aimed at teenagers. This means that difficult topics are dealt with sensitively and that hard concepts are broken down so that they become understandable. Equally, Newsround is not as long as a normal news bulletin, nor is it quite as upsetting or depressing. Therefore, it is the perfect resource to share with students. Additionally, it is a BBC show, so trustworthy, and not likely to be blocked by any oversensitive school filters!

You are unlikely to watch Newsround every single day – there simply is not the time. However, it is a great time filler, if you have a few minutes spare at the end of a tutor time. Equally, you may want to show it to students at the end of the week to wrap up the week that has just been. This is especially good if you decide to introduce the end of the week quiz with your tutor groups as well – Newsround suddenly acts as a revision tool and students really will sit up and pay attention.

Moreover, if you are moving towards a more structured and planned tutor time, then watching Newsround is the perfect choice for cover work. For example, if a tutor group is working through some of the revision strategies or maybe due to having a homework catch-up, this will be very hard for cover to do – especially if they are external to the school body. Therefore, to avoid wasting time and ensuring that you do not just have a wasted 20, 30, 40 minutes etc. of tutor time in any given day, Newsround becomes the perfect high-quality thing to leave, which is both easy 'cover' to set and very easy for whoever is covering the tutor group to pull up and share with students.

Debates

Students are always getting into arguments. Someone has taken something, someone said this, someone has threatened to do that, this person did this on the football pitch. Students really are great at getting into squabbles. This top tip suggests we should harness that ability to squabble by introducing debates into our classrooms.

Debating is an extremely difficult skill. How do you take on board the opinion of others? How do you avoid talking over them? How do you challenge someone respectfully? How can you trust your own sources of information or those of the people challenging you? Do you know a way to draw a debate to a close?

How many times in day-to-day life do we have a discussion or debate with someone and it feels like we are not being listened to or that someone is just not open to having their opinion and chain of thought challenged? All the time, right? And it is infuriating! Through developing the debating skills of students, it will improve their ability to take on board the opinions of others, challenge politely and respectfully, and justify their decisions and beliefs. And I think we would all be appreciative of this!

But there's more. By choosing the correct topics to debate, we can ensure that we can get students focusing on real-world topics, again making them more aware of the current affairs which are afflicting people locally and internationally. By challenging students to debate some big issues, we are also making sure that they are being forced to engage with these topics, and hopefully form an opinion, rather than passively watching some news or reading an article. It also provides that wonderful outlet for a squabble, too.

Introducing debates into tutor time is perfectly possible, so long as there are ground rules. Students need to know to take it in turns, how to challenge respectfully and how to refer to one another, for example. It will be worth sitting down with your colleagues and deciding on some rules for how this will run. You may already be lucky enough to have a debating club in school – if you do, what rules do they have? Additionally, if you do have a debating club in school, may it be possible for members of the debating club to model to students how they ought to conduct themselves in a debate (in the same way that we would model to students during a lesson too). Maybe a member of the debating club could even sit in with each tutor group when they do their first debate to help guide the process.

A little planning will be required to carry out these debates during tutor time. First, you will need to ensure that you pick appropriate topics – going straight in on the future relations of Israel and Palestine may not be too wise. You also need to ensure that it is something that students would have a little knowledge of or interest in, in order to be able to debate. If students have no interest, they won't do the research required for the debate, let alone actively get involved with the debate. When choosing debate topics, you may want to tie some of it in with the PSHE curriculum. This not only means that you are doing some great cross-curricular work, but you will likely be able to find some debate guidance and resources from everything that is available online for PSHE teaching. Finally, and as noted just above, students will need to take time to prepare for the debate. How you do this will be up to you, as well as choosing which side of the debate students sit on.

With a bit of planning, and reflection on how it goes the first few times, introducing debates to tutor time is a superb way of improving engagement with crucial current affairs issues. And who knows, you will spark the enthusiasm to form a debate club (or grow it if you have it), and maybe even enter local and national competitions, of which there are many!

Social Action

This top tip considers how you can utilise tutor time in order to provide students with the opportunity to potentially get involved with social action. The top tips so far have focused more on making students aware of international issues. But students also need to be aware of what is happening in their local community as well. And where they want and are able, they ought to get involved with local social action as well.

Examples of social action that students may wish to get involved in include:

- Homelessness
- Food banks
- Play areas
- Playing fields
- Youth clubs
- Opportunities in the local community
- Support for OAPs
- Road safety

The issues that students really care about will be dependent on the local community, as well as their own upbringing and experiences. Regardless of the student, there will be something that they care about in their local area.

Getting students involved in social action is a wonderful way of getting them involved in the community, something which can all too often be lacking. Students have the ideas and energy to be able to make massively positive impacts in a lot of these areas. Additionally, and maybe more for the individual, getting involved in social action is great for skills building, and would be great evidence for a lot of students when they get to producing a CV or when they are at an interview. It's also a required component of schemes such as the Duke of Edinburgh's Award.

It may be that students do not go out and complete this social action work during a tutor time – this could be extremely difficult unless a local charity or organisation either comes into the school or is doing work right next door (which is not impossible). However, tutor time provides an opportunity for you to lead students on considering local issues and things that they care about, and then finding groups that they can get involved with who are actively working on these issues. Students are unlikely to even know that social action exists, let alone how to get involved with it, so we can be the helping hand in getting them active in the community.

School Council

Having covered international affairs and local affairs, this top tip now moves on to affairs at school – through the introduction, or improvement, of your school council. School councils are not a new thing, but they may also not be the most effectively run thing in your school, either.

Let us consider the purpose of the school council. Primarily, it provides an opportunity to get feedback from students. What is going well? What is not going so well? Where do student priorities lie? Moving past this, the student council also provides an opportunity to get groups of students actually getting on with projects. For example, if one area of the field is not up to scratch, then can the council get a group of students together to get the work done on it that needs doing? Additionally, for those on the council, it provides a superb opportunity to develop a number of characteristics, including presenting, working with others, planning, organisation, communication and leadership. More generally, the school community is able to witness democracy in action, ensuring that students are made aware of the process of campaigning and voting, as they will be exposed to in later life.

As this will not be a new top tip to anyone, rather than telling you how to go about setting up a school council, as it will already likely exist, here are some questions that will hopefully challenge you as to how well the school council is being run:

- Do non-council members get an opportunity to raise concerns to their tutor group representatives?
- How many members of staff are made aware of what the school council are working on, what they are saying is working well, and the areas that need improvement?
- Are the school council active in leading projects?
- Do the school council meet frequently enough to raise new concerns and follow up on previous ones?
- Is there a member of staff who is given the time required to lead the student council effectively as well as provide feedback to the required members of staff after meetings have taken place?
- Is tutor time used effectively to get students to come together for student council and lead on projects?
- Do non-council members ever get updates on what the student council is doing?

There are a huge number of things that can improve the way that a school council is run. No school council is perfect, so take some time to consider what you are already doing, and how things can be improved yet further!

Litter Picking and Tree Planting

Though the student council may eventually get around to proposing and leading on some projects in school, there is no reason why there can be pre-determined social action opportunities that all students can get involved with at school – namely, litter picking and tree planting.

Both of these opportunities provide students with a way of getting involved with important actions that improve the school site that they go to. Both are also brilliant ways of supporting the environment, and both will support the local community too. They're easier to organise as well, because tutor groups across all year groups can be put on a rota to complete these two tasks. Across all of the years in a school, that probably means that each tutor group would do one litter pick and one tree planting session per half-term, which really is not that many when the significantly positive action of these activities is considered.

Both are fairly affordable too. A few buckets and little pickers wouldn't cost too much, whilst tree saplings are often available on deals for schools – and that is if they even cost at all. Bulbs and seeds are also often available, again for very low costs or completely free from local charities and organisations.

By getting students involved in both of these activities, they will be giving back to their school community, and making their school a better place to go each day to learn. You may even inspire students to get involved with social action outside school because of this action that they are taking in school. There are so many local community gardens and tree planting projects to start with – so make sure you have an idea of when these are. Maybe this could be something that students even find out about themselves and then share in the newsletter that they are helping to produce (as per one of the previous top tips).

Charity Work

It has been mentioned a few times in this book, but getting students involved with charity work at school is a great thing to do. So often there are charity events being run at school, but how much of this is actually organised by the students? Are the charities that are being supported chosen by the students? Do they get to decide what activities to run? In a few circumstances they will, but let us consider how charity work at school can be done even better!

First, is it possible for students in a school year, within their tutor groups, to decide on a charity that they want to support that year? You may have a school charity, but equally there are likely to be different charities which really appeal to students. You might want to give students a selection of charities to choose from, or maybe you can just let them suggest different charities that they care about? It may even be that each tutor group decides on a charity and then they put forward the case for them, but then the year group votes on the overall favourite.

Second, can students determine the events that they are going to run? Could, for example, each different tutor group be responsible for one specific event. And by responsible, this includes:

- Deciding on the event
- Planning the event
- Completing all paperwork on an event
- Running the event
- Staffing the event as required

Within your tutor group, students could be put into small sub groups who all have their own area of responsibility. Some might be in charge of advertising, some may do the paperwork, some may talk an assembly about what they are doing – and so forth!

Third, students should be responsible for the evaluation of their events. Did they make as much money as they thought? What went well? What are they going to do differently next time?

All of these three stages can be coordinated through a tutor time. If tutors are clear on what needs to be done, and the deadlines and processes for it, then it would be possible for them to supervise all of these stages and guide students along them. Think of all of the benefits to the students of doing this – the communication, the teamwork, the additional responsibilities that they would face. Getting students involved in organising charity fundraising at school is a wonderful way to get them involved in things that they care about and improve a large number of 'soft skills'.

Key Issue Presentations

The penultimate tip top for this section is a way to get students talking about issues that they are passionate about. As you will have gathered in this section, the aim is to get students enthused in issues locally, domestically and internationally. This, however, is forgetting that students are probably already enthusiastic about a huge number of different issues. Just because we don't necessarily recognise them as big topics, or things that are relevant to us in our adult lives, does not mean that they are not key issues for our students.

One way in which to tap into this is to get students to give a presentation on a topic that they really care about. You have two choices here – you either let a few students volunteer to do this (but are any going to want to do that?) or you make it something compulsory for every student in the tutor group. I would go for the latter, and then reduce the amount of time that students need to talk for.

You will need to give students some guidelines on how to produce and deliver their presentation, but try to give them as much individuality about the topic they are talking about as possible. If students are struggling, you may need to give them some support, maybe getting them to think about what they talk to their friends about or debates they have around sport or celebrities, for example. It really does not matter what students want to talk about, as long as they actually do it! You may need to mandate if the presentation is on PowerPoint or if one is actually needed at all, and you should probably give students a time limit (or target) as well. Beyond this, try to give students as much space for individual creativity as possible.

To get all students in a tutor group completed, you will probably need to do one presentation a week, or for smaller tutor groups, one every other week. If the presentations are only 1–2 minutes long though, this should not be too much of a commitment. You will need to give up some time for students to make their presentations, but again, not too much planning should be needed for such a small presentation. A couple of tutor blocks across a term should be more than enough, and if you do use the computer room rota top tip, a couple of sessions in there should be plenty for students to get everything completed.

This top tip offers a great opportunity for students to improve their research and presentation skills, but mainly gives them a space and an audience to talk about something that they care about. They may connect with others who really care about those issues too, and at worst, you will find out a little bit more about what makes your tutees tick! This sounds like a win win!

Inspirational Speakers

The final top tip for this section, and it is all about inspiration! We have all read those (cheesy) inspirational quotes, and probably watched our fair share of inspirational speakers too. The ones which I find hit home are when people really have a story to tell – an upbringing to explain, barriers they broke down and difficulties that they faced.

This tip suggests that it is a really good idea to expose students to as many of these as possible, due to the huge range of benefits it has. First, students will get to see the struggles that others have been through and the successes that they have had. For some students, this will be the first time that struggles of that ilk will have been shown to them – it can really help to show them the privileges that they have – for example free education. But equally, a lot of these videos are likely to chime with the difficulties that students them-selves have faced, for example if they are young carers. These videos can offer some inspiration as to what they are able to go on and achieve regardless of their background.

Furthermore, a lot of these inspirational speakers talk of many of the key current affairs in the world, as that is often what has impacted them so very much. Again, getting students watching these speakers will open students' eyes to what is really happening out there in the 'real world' – again, no bad thing.

As a staff body, you are all likely to have certain speakers or speeches that really inspire you. Perhaps these could be collated and then over the course of several terms be shared with students. It may seem repetitive, but it is never a bad thing to have an inspirational talk!

If you are lucky – perhaps monetarily, location wise or depending on old students – you may even be able to get an inspirational speaker to come into school. Something like this can really capture a student's imagination, and last long in their memories when they look back on good times in school. This is not going to be something that you do all of the time, but if you are able to get a, or a few inspirational speakers into school over the course of an academic year, that really could be wonderful for everyone involved in your school community.

8 Wellbeing

The final chapter of this book is around the area of wellbeing. Mental health is a priority in schools now, as is more widespread student wellbeing, especially when it comes to anxiety and pressures of exams. Beyond this, though, is the importance of a healthy work-life, or rather, school-life balance, and ensuring that students are able to switch off from the pressures of school life, and are generally healthy, physically, and mentally. With limited time, resources, and often expertise, how do we go about this in schools? Equally, where major changes like removing exams are not possible, what are the small things that we can do in school to help students not only cope, but also thrive in the structure in which we find ourselves?

The aim of this chapter is to give you a range of strategies which can support the mental health and wellbeing of our young people, whilst also complementing the strategies provided in the other chapters of this book, allowing them to seamless fit into the tutor time curriculum you will be building.

Mindfulness

We know that students often struggle to self-regulate their behaviours, often bringing in stresses and worries from home, from

DOI: 10.4324/9781003605881-9

their previous lesson or even from something that has just happened at a breaktime or lunchtime. Ideally, we want our students to be able to regulate their emotions, and be prepared for the next activity at hand, usually a lesson.

One of the ways in which this can be done is through the introduction of mindfulness lessons. Mindfulness provides students with a range of strategies that they can utilise in order to regulate: their breathing, body, and general behaviours. It isn't a strategy that will work for all students, but it could potentially work for a handful within each tutor group. However, if students have never been informed of, and taught how to be mindful, then it is not something that they will then be able to go and do independently.

Sometimes mindfulness is already included within more general PSE lessons, but where it isn't, it could provide one option for a wellbeing session, that could be done, for example, once per week or fortnight. It may be that you decide to get an expert in from the local area, or possibly utilise the skills of one member of teaching staff. If you don't have this expertise at your fingertips, then you could do worse than carefully selecting a few quality videos from websites such as YouTube.

How you run this could vary. It could be done on a tutor group by tutor group basis, or you may decide to get the whole year group together in order to do it. Equally, a mindfulness session may be a one-off session that you run, re-visited once per term, or possibly run for a few weeks in a row so that students can practice and master a number of techniques that they are able to use, whenever required, in their lives.

A further point of consideration is that we know that students can sometimes be a little big giggly. Before doing a session like this, ensure that expectations are set, that boundaries are put into place, and that a positive culture has been established along with a rationale for the importance of the session. As suggested above, these techniques may not work for all students, but it will work for some.

Stress Sessions

Stresses in school are like nothing else. The pressure that students face with assessments – even just end of topic tests in Year 7 – seem huge. We've all seen students worried about these types of assessments, where we know that the stakes are low and that they really don't need to be getting themselves into such a panic. Equally, where stakes are high, as they are in Year 11 and Year 13, we still don't want students to be too stressed. As we'll be aware, a little bit of stress is good to get us working, but too much stress is a negative thing – both mentally and physically.

Therefore, one of our options is to train students around stress. What are the different types of stress? How do they impact us? What stress could we define as 'healthy stress' and what stress should be raising some 'red flags'? On top of this, we also need students to have a range of techniques to be able to handle stress; things that they can do which alleviate some of the pressure that they are feeling.

One option is to directly address these concerns by having stress wellbeing sessions. One of the ways this can be done is through organising for a local charity or organisation who specialise in this area to come in and deliver a session around this. One of the very best sessions I attended allowed students to identify what types of stress there were, understand where they may be on the scale, and what they could do if their own stress levels were too high. It was a superb session allowing for students to begin to regulate their stress levels far better.

If there aren't any organisations available in your local area, there are a wealth of high-quality, student focused resources on line, such as those by YoungMinds or even the NHS. One option would be to get students to research this area, and then present back to their tutor group. Or perhaps a tutor group could be split into smaller groups, and then they all research stress around exams and coping with it, and then compare notes.

With this type of activity, it will also be wise to have signposts to services that are available for students, both within school, if you have any, and those outside school. It'll also be a time where safeguarding concerns may arise, so be aware of those as well.

This type of activity is more likely to be a one off, but it would be wise to consider whether having it is in Year 7, and not just a few months before exams in Year 11, would be wise. Students in younger years still face stress, as outlined at the start of this strategy. Perhaps this workshop, or whatever format you devise, could be re-run each year so that students can remind themselves of healthy and unhealthy stress, and how to deal with the latter? Leaving it to Year 11 feels a little late!

Mental Health Education

Mental health has possibly never been a more pressing matter than post-COVID. Add in the world of social media, and the chaos and stress that this causes, along with exams and the general difficulties of teenage life, along with overstretched services, and it is easy to see why we have such a crisis for our young people. Most schools are already doing a huge amount around mental health, including training staff up to be mental health leaders, or having a designated member of staff to support students.

Really, there should be a whole section on mental-health within this book, but space limits it to just a point. Therefore, this strategy will raise a number of ways that we can support students with their mental health, through the tutor programme.

- Get a tutor group, or a whole year group, to lead an assembly on mental health. This could include the different things to look out for, services that are available and things that you can do in school to support others.
- Consider introducing 'kindness days', or similar, where all students are forced to consider the situation that other students are facing, and thus reflect on the language that they are using with others.
- Ensure that students are clear on the individuals and services that they are able to reach out to, both within schools, and outside school. Again, this may lead to some safeguarding issues being raised, so do be aware.
- You could select inspirational talks from individuals who have been through difficult times with their mental health, but are on the road for improvement. Carefully selected videos, that are age and student appropriate, will need to be chosen, of course.
- Each tutor group could elect a mental health spokesperson for the tutor group. These individuals could then meet together, a little like the school council, and discuss plans for school and raise any issues that need to be raised. This would be an opportunity for the school council, and the wider school leadership team, to hear from students around any issues in school impacting mental health, or equally, things that are going well.
- Mental health should be covered through the PSE curriculum, but where more time is needed, tutor time would be a suitable opportunity to share more of these resources and activities with students, to improve their understanding of wider mental health and steps that they can take to improve their own mental health.
- Ensure that you are utilising sufficient wellbeing strategies, including some of those listed within this chapter, so that students have sufficient opportunity to work on their own self-regulation and mental health.

Maximising Tutor Time

- Utilise the resources developed by the Department for Education around improving mental health in schools. Further resources can also be found through organisations such as Mentally Healthy Schools.

There will be a large number of other things that you could do, and may already be doing, to support the mental health of students during tutor time. The list above is not exclusive, but will hopefully provide you with further ideas of activities that you can build into your tutor programme in order to support mental health in your schools.

Outdoor Opportunities

Nature is an undervalued consideration when it comes to wellbeing. I would challenge anyone to tell me a time where they have been out in nature and haven't felt better for it! However, when we are in school, it is very easy to be trapped within four walls all day long. In fact, if you don't go outside during a break or lunch, it is possible to not see any sunlight for a whole school day (an upsetting fact that I am sure all too many teachers are aware of when we get to the winter months).

Therefore, this strategy proposes that, where suitable and possible, tutor time is held outside. Of course, many of the activities that we want to do need to be within a classroom, because we need computers, desks or equipment. However, there are plenty of activities that can be done outside, including many of the enrichment ones listed earlier on in the book, and many of these wellbeing strategies, too.

If you do decide to hold some tutor time sessions outside, then I would recommend that you explain the benefits of being outdoors to students, which include:

- Supports mental health
- Supports physical health
- Improves sleep quality
- Supports creativity
- Supports immunity
- Reduces worry
- Improves mood
- Supports self-confidence
- Reduces loneliness
- Helps you to connect to nature

It may even be that you don't translate an indoor activity into an outdoor one. Instead, you enjoy nature, and just go for a walk. Perhaps there is a local nature reserve or large park near you that you could go an enjoy, or even school fields further away from the building so that you can have some air?

All of these opportunities provide students with a chance, that they may not otherwise have, to enjoy and experience nature. Our lives are incredibly busy, as are those of our students. Social media can dominate, and enjoying the world around us can often take a backseat. Providing this opportunity to enjoy nature – or even point it out to students(!) – is a super way of opening up new opportunities and supporting the wellbeing of our students.

Turn and Talk

As has been mentioned several times already in this chapter is the dominance of social media in the lives of our students. Gone are the days of knocking on for a friend afterschool and just playing in the street. Now, messaging and viral videos are the thing. This has a significant impact on an individual's ability to just have a general conversation, though. If you are constantly messaging and sending reels, rather than going out to play with friends, when do you actually learn how to have (and enjoy) a conversation with someone else?

This strategy proposes that you actually timetable in opportunities for students to talk. This could be done in a couple of ways:

1. Students are allowed to go and sit next to whichever student, or students they want to, and then just talk. There are no out-of-bounds topics (unless they become significantly inappropriate, of course), but anything from family life to football, to pets and latest adventures is on the cards! Join in with conversations where you want, and enjoy getting to know your students a little bit better. The time will fly by, and students will have a great opportunity to have some really good, in-depth conversations with their friends.
2. You determine student pairs, and provide them with some topics of conversation. Going about the activity in this way is of course more difficult – you are likely to face resistance, and students are more likely to struggle when they get into conversations. Therefore, you are likely to only go about this activity in this way if you are directly looking to improve students' communication abilities, rather than just general wellbeing. In this method, it would be appropriate to give students questions or points of discussion to ease their chat, and possibly provide a short time limit so it doesn't seem too overwhelming.

There are a huge number of benefits to introducing conversation as a more regular part of tutor time, including:

*   Improve student's oracy abilities
*   Improve students listening abilities
*   Improving student's abilities to hold a conversation
*   Allowing students to develop more in-depth (or less superficial!), conversations

- Provide the opportunity for new friendships to form
- Provide some 'down-time' before a busy school day, or at the end of a long day!

Introducing this within my own tutor time was one of the best things that I ever did, and I really would urge you to give it a go, above and beyond many of the other strategies mentioned in this book. It truly is a favourite of mine!

Plan a Social

Building on the above idea is that of planning a social. You are likely to have a lot of friendships within your tutor group, either previously formed, or perhaps newly formed through activities like the conversation one above. Again, building from the idea that students spend a significant portion of time on social media rather than physically with each other, is this idea that students plan a social for their tutor group, where they will spend time with each other doing an activity.

It is likely that you will utilise this strategy in the run up to a holiday, often Christmas, Easter or Summer; at the end of a long term where everyone is quite tired. The emphasis here is on formally planning an activity, rather than just scrambling something together the day before, or the day of, a tutor time (for example, throwing a film on as it is 'something different', but actually only half of the students want to watch and even then, you do not actually have the time to finish it off over the course of a few tutor periods!). Ensure that you identify the date, or dates, that you can have your socials on, and get planning early. You'll of course need to use a few tutor periods up, but if you have a blocked out 'wellbeing' session each week or fortnight, then this should give you the time to do it.

Maximising Tutor Time

It is up to students what they want to do, and they will likely be creative, but a few ideas to get you started:

- Board games
- Cake and hot chocolate
- Crafting
- Charades
- Bingo
- Quizzes
- Festive related activities

Some of these activities of course require a little more planning, for example the cake and hot chocolate, but all are perfectly do-able with a little bit of planning, and a superb way for your students to have some social down time, enjoying activities and each other's company!

Personal Reflections

The final strategy provided in this section is the opportunity for students to record down their personal reflections. A huge part of wellbeing is students being able to take time to consider how it is they are feeling: the things which are making them happy, or sad; the worries that they face or the excitement that they have. It is often easier to reflect on these thoughts where they are written down, as reflecting upon them whilst they are just sitting within your internal monologue is incredibly difficult (the cognitive strain!).

In many ways, this strategy is almost like students keeping a personal diary (which I feel has much gone out of fashion). One way in which to do this is to provide students with a small reporter's notebook, where each small page can be the day in which students are recording down their notes. Alternatively, students may have sections within their homework diary, if this is something that you have in school, where they would be able to write down reflections.

As this strategy requires time to be given to it more frequently, it may be something that you wish to build in to every tutor time. Perhaps the first 2 minutes of each session provide an opportunity for students to record down anything that they would like to in their personal reflections?

It should also be noted, that to begin with, students are likely going to struggle with completing their personal reflections. What on earth do they write down? As with everything else that we teach students, it would be wise to model it to them (perhaps with your own reflections on the day or the week), and then provide some guidance points for students to consider when wondering what to write down. These points provide a strong scaffold that, in time, can hopefully be removed.

Positively, by utilising this strategy, we are up-skilling our students with an approach that can support them in multiple aspects of their life, both within school when reflecting on behaviour, academic pursuits and self-regulation, but also when they are at home, too. It is an approach – pausing and writing down your thoughts and feelings – which can be incredibly powerful for a lot of adults, and thus sets our students up very well for future life.

Conclusion

There we have it. A number of different, high-quality strategies across eight different areas, all with the potential, if implemented effectively and coherently, to significantly improve the outcomes of students in our schools, measured in a number of different ways, but including behaviour, attainment and attendance.

Tutor time continues to provide us with a significant block of time each school week, which too often is a dumping ground for 'other' activities. Through determining whole-school priorities, as well as identifying key areas for student development, a range of strategies can be selected from this book in order to turn tutor time into a vehicle for significant student development, each and every day.

Good luck!

 DOI: 10.4324/9781003605881-10

Index

academic: improvement 1–3, 74, 106–107; pursuits 123
activities: further ideas of 118; type of 116
afterschool 19–20, 87–88, 119
allotment 99–100
anti-bullying week 31–33
anxiety 113
artistic opportunities 56
assemblies 7–8
assessments, types of 115
attainment 1–2, 5, 74, 79, 86, 88, 124
attendance 1–3, 5, 15–18, 124
awareness: AIDS 35; of anti-bullying week 32; raising 31

behaviour 11, 22, 52–53, 71–72, 76, 85, 113–114, 123–124; conversations 13–15; general 114; out-of-lesson 18; policy 6
Black History Month 28–30, 40
brain 69, 97–98
Brilliant Club 87–88
buddy-up system 90–91

careers activities 80–81
charity 96–97, 108–110

Children in Need 33–35
Christmas celebrations 35
clear message communication 24–25
cognitive: loads 1, 68–69; planning 59
communication 42, 106, 109, 120
community gardens 108
competition 45–46, 53, 55
computer access 81–82
contracts, setting and checking 22–24
conversations 14–15, 48, 53, 121; attendance 15–16; behaviour 13–15; benefits to introducing 120–121; mobile phone 17–18; points of 50–51; transformational 15; in tutor time 47
course: activities of 122; reflections of 49
creativity 3; description of 44; famous events on this day 51–53; famous people born on this day 50–51; general knowledge quizzes 53–54; house competitions 55–56; Poem of the Day 44–46; prayer for the day 48–49; quizzes 54–55; religious passage for the day 49–50; shapes and sizes 56;

Index

thought for the day 47–48; word of the day 46–47
CREST 86–87
cross-curricular links 53, 63
current affairs 3; charity work 108–110; debates 103–104; description of 101; inspirational speakers 111–112; key issue presentations 110–111; litter picking and tree planting 107–108; school council 106–107; social action 104–106; watch Newsround 101–102
curriculum 4, 9, 45–47, 57, 59, 83, 92

debates 103–104
Department for Education 96, 118
detentions 6, 18–21, 23
development 4, 14, 36, 44, 46–47, 124
Duke of Edinburgh's Award 105

EEF 58
election campaigns 101
emotions 114
English intervention 74–75
Enhanced Project Qualification (EPQ) 79
enrichment 3, 78–80, 118; allotment 99–100; description of 92; green activities 96–97; language sessions 93–94; music lessons 94–96; newsletters 97–99; opportunity for 78; options 87; sports 92–93
environment/environmental 47, 65; impact 96–97; issues 97
equipment checks 12–13
evaluation strategies 59
events: anti-bullying week 31–33; Black History Month 28–30; Children in Need 33–35; description of 28; Pride Month 40–41; Remembrance Day 30–31; Safer Internet Day 36–37; school specific celebrations 42–43; St Andrews/St Davids/St George and St Patrick's Day 37–38; student idols 41–42; World AIDS Day 35–36; World Refugee Day 39–40

Events of the Year 2; see also events
exams, anxiety and pressures of 113
extra-curricular activities 66–67

faculty led interventions 76–77
faith schools 49
feedback 57, 87, 107
fingertip facts 63–64
flashcards 60, 62
free education 111
fundraising 33–34

GCSE 44, 62, 71, 74, 77–78, 84–85, 89, 94
graduation 87
group discussions 52

habit forming 67–68
Head of Year (HoY) Interventions 18–20
high-quality tutor programme 57
homework 63–67, 71–72, 81; diaries 66; follow-up 25–26; interventions 82–83; recording platforms 66
house competitions 56

inspirational speakers 111–112
interventions 3; additional GCSEs 77–78; benefits for running 83–84; Brilliant Club 87–88; buddy-up system 90–91; careers activities 80–81; computer access 81–82; CREST 86–87; description of 73; English 75; enrichment 78–80; faculty led 76–77; homework 82–83; mentoring 88–89; mixed year group support 83–84; numeracy 74; SEN workshops see SEN workshops
IT issues 26–27

key issue presentations 110–111
knowledge 44, 53–54, 59, 60, 63–64

language 44–47, 93–94
leadership 14, 16–17, 58, 77, 106

learning, developing 3, 53, 68–69;
    description of 57; environment
    70; fingertip facts 63–64; habit
    forming 67–68; homework 64–67;
    metacognition sessions 58–60;
    processes 67–68; revision 60–63;
    schemes of 52; silent reading
    71–72; working environment 69–70
LGBTQ community 40–41
literacy 47, 71
litter picking 107–108
local charity 115
long-term memory 68–69

mental health 8, 113, 116; education
    116–118; leaders 116; in schools
    118; of students 118
mentoring 88–89
messaging 2, 119; attendance
    conversations 15–16; behaviour
    conversations 13–15; clear
    message communication 24–25;
    description of 6; equipment
    checks 12–13; Head of Year
    Interventions 18–20; homework
    follow-up 25–26; IT issues 26–27;
    mobile phone conversations
    17–18; pick up students for
    detention 20–21; pick up students
    for isolation 21–22; practising
    routines 9–11; school assemblies
    7–8; setting and checking
    contracts 22–24; SLT drop-ins
    16–17; uniform checks 11–12;
    workshops 8–9
metacognition sessions 58–60
mindfulness 113–115
mobile phone conversations 17–18
Modern Foreign Language (MFL)
    93–94
monitoring 13, 22, 58, 59
music lessons 94–96

National Curriculum 1
nature 118–119
Newsround 101–102
newsletters 97–99

non-financial rewards 55
numeracy intervention 74

OpenLearn platform 79
opportunity for enrichment 94–96
oppression, awareness of 40
organisation 30, 32, 65, 87, 106,
    108, 115, 118

parental meetings 1
persistent absenteeism 18
personal reflections 122–123
pick up students: for detention
    20–21; for isolation 21–22
picking strategies 59
planning 58–59, 62, 78, 81, 106,
    122; of homework 65; social
    121–122
poetry 44–46, 55
positive culture 114–115
PowerPoint presentation 66–67, 69
presentation 48, 69, 110–111; for
    students 70; PowerPoint 66–67, 69
Pride Month 40–41
problem-solving type styles 59
PSE/H: curriculum 104, 116; delivery
    79; lessons 114; teaching 104

qualifications 78–80
questioning 51–52
quiz/quizzes 53–56

reading 41, 49–50, 60, 71–72, 75,
    88, 103
red flags 115
reflections 122–123
Remembrance Day 30–31
resources 29, 35, 69, 84, 100, 104, 117
revision 60–61; effective 60;
    skills 62–63; strategy 61–63;
    techniques 57
routines, practising 9–11

Safer Internet Day 36–37
secondary school 33, 41, 85
self-regulation 116, 123
self-testing strategies 62, 64

Index

semi-regular computer access 81–82
SEN students 59
Senior Leadership Team 80
short-term memory 68
silent reading 71–72
skills 90, 114
SLT 8, 16–18
social media 47, 119, 121; viral
  videos 119
soft skills 110
speaking 13–14
Special Education Needs
  (SEN) workshops 84; access
  arrangements 84–85; assessments
  85; behaviour plans 85–86; lesson
  access plans 86
sports 92–93
St Andrews/St Davids/St George and
  St Patrick's Day 37–38
staff development 46–47
Stonewall resources 41
strategies 3–5, 59, 61–64, 118,
  120–123
stress 113–116; healthy 115–116;
  unhealthy 116
subject specific vocabulary 46

teachers 60, 69, 76
timetable 2, 4, 53, 71, 74

transportation issues 87
tree planting 107–108
Triple Science 77–78
tutor time 1, 19, 62–65, 76–77,
  85–86, 102, 109, 121, 124;
  checks 13; curriculum 44, 73;
  programme 4, 73
tutor/tutoring 1, 15–16, 63–64;
  groups 32, 54, 76, 81–82,
  114, 116; length of period 50;
  programme 29, 40, 61, 116, 118;
  timetable 71, 74

uniform checks 11–12

wellbeing 3, 121–122; description
  of 113; mental health
  education 116–118; mindfulness
  113–115; of students 119; outdoor
  opportunities 118–119; personal
  reflections 122–123; planning a
  social 121–122; strategies 116;
  stress sessions 115–116; turn and
  talk 119–121
working environment
  69–70, 82
workshops 8–9, 116
World AIDS Day 35–36
World Refugee Day 39–40